3418253

WITHDRAWN
NDSU

Out in the Mid-day Sun

Out in
the Mid-day Sun

BY

BORIS GUSSMAN

London
GEORGE ALLEN & UNWIN LTD
RUSKIN HOUSE MUSEUM STREET

FIRST PUBLISHED IN 1962

This book is copyright under the Berne Convention. Apart from any fair dealing for the purposes of private study, research, criticism or review, as permitted under the Copyright Act, 1956, no portion may be reproduced by any process without written permission. Enquiries should be addressed to the publisher.

©   *George Allen & Unwin Ltd., 1962*

DT
853
U8
1962 b

PRINTED IN GREAT BRITAIN

in 10 point Baskerville

BY WILLMER BROTHERS AND HARAM LTD
BIRKENHEAD

Preface

The problem of Africa is the African. This has seemed to many people for many years to have been the case. Yet there is mounting evidence that there is a European problem just as complex and in every way as intractible. Many of us in England still find this proposal difficult to accept. We take the Englishman in the multi-racial areas of East and Central Africa for granted. He is one of us. At the same time, his behaviour, behaviour that many of us criticize, often seems incomprehensible, and we make the easy assumption that we would behave differently. How, people sometimes ask, can these primarily British settlers so readily align themselves with the forces of racial prejudice? How can they accept the pass law system, the segregation of residential areas, the many and varied restrictive practices that characterize the scene in Central Africa today? Why is their behaviour so different to our own? Does the situation create the man or does man create the situation?

There is no easy answer. Certainly, when the three British Central African territories of Southern Rhodesia, Northern Rhodesia and Nyasaland were linked together to form the Federation of Rhodesia and Nyasaland in 1953, many people believed that a new era in inter-racial partnership had dawned. It was felt that the European settlers would now have the chance to demonstrate their progressive liberal tendencies under a Constitution that was seen as a compromise between the rabid white nationalism of the South and the possible dangers of Black nationalism to the North.

These high hopes have not been realized and the Africans have looked in vain for concrete examples of true partnership. Disillusion has set in and has been followed by bitterness and hostility. The European settlers for their part genuinely believe that they are bringing the Africans on as fast as is consistent with efficiency, integrity and prudence and they roundly condemn them for their apparent ingratitude.

As a result, relations between the two major races have grown increasingly bitter and there are in the main two reasons for this trend. The first derives from the activities of the politicians and the second from personal problems of adjustment that both European settlers and indigenous Africans meet in different forms.

On the political front there is a fair measure of British Government responsibility. A situation has been allowed to develop in British Central Africa that is very similar in many respects to the position in Palestine at the time of the Mandate. Promises, or assurances that were readily interpreted as promises, have been given by successive

British Governments to both Europeans and Africans and a conflict of rights has arisen. For the Africans, there was initially the Doctrine of Paramountcy, first promulgated by the Duke of Devonshire in 1923. The significant passage in this document read, 'His Majesty's Government think it necessary definitely to record their considered opinion that the interests of African Natives must be paramount, and that if and when these interests and those of the immigrant races should conflict, the former should prevail.'

At the time when this Declaration was made the Africans were politically dormant and they paid it little heed. It was also largely ignored by the European settlers, few if any of whom were thinking in those days of a permanent home in Central Africa. But when Lord Passmore, the Labour Party's Secretary of State for the Colonies, re-stated the proposition in 1930, the seeds for discord were well and truly sown. By then Africans were beginning to think in terms of nationalism. The Europeans for their part had just come through the economic crisis of the late 1920's. They were beginning to feel their feet again. Indeed they were beginning to seek a permanent foothold in the territory and they strongly resented the implications behind the Declaration.

How far the idea of African paramountcy could have been applied to Southern Rhodesia is uncertain. Since 1923 the country had enjoyed a fair measure of autonomy but the British Government had reserved to itself a veto on any legislation affecting African interests. African paramountcy could possibly have been argued in the British Parliament although, in fact, it never has been brought up in relation to Southern Rhodesia.

Despite the Declaration of Paramountcy, the European Settlers in Central Africa have through the years been given assurances by successive Governments in Britain that their property, their security and their continued occupation would be guaranteed. These assurances culminated in the creation of the Federation in 1953. With the founding of this new State, paramountcy of Africa interests was dead and racial partnership became the official policy. The Africans, however, have nonetheless continued to base their case for independence upon the Devonshire Declaration and as they had no say in the creation of the Federation in any case, they feel that they have a fair measure of right on their side. In this they have a considerable amount of sympathy and support, not only in Britain itself, but also internationally.

This book does not attempt to discuss the political manoeuvring that has occurred over the past thirty years. On these issues there is already a considerable literature and little is left to be said. Much too has also been written about the Africans, particularly by the anthropologists, although very little useful work has been done on those

Africans who have left the tribal areas and settled down to a form of urban domestication. Relations between the races have been dealt with extensively by many authors. But almost nothing at all has been written about the Europeans themselves and the problems they face. There is, therefore, a serious gap in our knowledge of the situation in Central Africa, and it is with this much neglected aspect that this book primarily concerns itself.

The European settlers have had a bad press of recent years. Their behaviour and in particular their attitude towards the Africans in whose midst they live has become increasingly the subject of adverse world criticism. Yet, in the light of our lack of knowledge about these Europeans it is pertinent to wonder how informed much of this criticism really is. Are those who condemn sure that they would behave any differently were they to find themselves in a similar situation? We just do not know. So it is with this in mind that I have tried to examine in the following pages how justified are the criticisms and why, if they are true, the European settler behave as they do.

As a start it is important to make the point that the behaviour of these Settlers cannot be understood in the context of Central Africa alone. Long before the Englishman set sail for India or Africa he had already shown, in his dealings with his subordinates, most of the faults for which the present-day Settlers are blamed. The owners of the dark satanic mills at the time of the Industrial Revolution, the merchant adventurers in India and the settlers in Central Africa all reveal much the same attitude to those they employed irrespective of race.

There are of course certain special local circumstances operating in Central Africa that did not occur either in eighteenth-century Britain or in nineteenth-century India. And of these special circumstances the African himself is the most important. His very numbers, his traditional way of looking at life, his inability to absorb Western civilization in a generation—all these exercise a considerable influence on European behaviour.

I do not want in any way to minimize the achievements of the settlers in the Federation but it will avail them little to have brought so many of the trappings of Western civilization to Africa if they fail to win the willing co-operation of the African people. And this, so far, they have utterly failed to do. This book is about the problems they face. It is not a record of their technical achievements.

Nothing can be done about past promises to either race, promises that in the circumstances of the twentieth century can no longer be implemented. But much can be done to improve the relations between the races. To achieve this improvement it is necessary to look very objectively at the whole situation, and when one does this it is impossible not to say some very harsh things about the white settlers.

These things have to be said nonetheless or there is a danger that one will miss or fail to understand the behaviour of both races.

This saying of harsh things would seem to be unfashionable in England today where, in our efforts not to be what we call crude and not to hurt anybody's feelings, we water down our opinions and understate our feelings to the extent that they have become insipid, trivial and we finish by influencing nobody. In this book I have tried not to understate. Nonetheless, wherever possible, I have quoted either from authoritative sources or given the opinions of people whose judgement can usually be accepted. Where possible also I have tried to give extenuating circumstances and indeed the argument behind the book is that the Englishmen who go overseas are not really very different to those who stay at home. If there is an ultimate culprit in the whole sad story it is human nature. That, however, does not make the problems any easier or mollify African opinion one little bit.

When discussing the Africans, I have drawn on my own experiences for most of the material. I have spent four of the past twelve years investigating problems of African detribalization and my enquiries have taken me over most of the Union of South Africa, the Rhodesias and Portuguese East Africa. This has enabled me to learn something at first hand of the domestic day-to-day difficulties of adjustment that Africans must face and overcome if they are to make the transition from the subsistence economy of tribal life to the highly individual monetary economy of the Western world. Few of these problems have been given very much attention in the past. In the main this is because they are in themselves quite trivial. Nobody considers, for example, that an African's clothes do not last so long as the same garments would if worn by Europeans because the African has to do all his washing in cold water. But trivial matters of this kind, if they are taken together, can add up to a quite considerable sum of frustration and embitterment.

Events in the Federation are moving fast. Strikes follow breakdowns in negotiations; there are outbreaks of violence followed by restrictive legislation followed by more violence; constitutional changes follow constitutional changes to the extent that any plan is already outdated before it is given a chance to work; troop movements, appeals to this or that political party in Britain, murder, arson and mob fury all follow so quickly the one upon the other that the writer faces an impossible task. He too is outdated before even the ink is dry. Only if he sticks to broad principles can he make any useful contribution. This I have tried to do and I have made little comment upon the day-to-day happenings that have kept the Federation on the front pages of the world's press.

On the whole the book deals with the relations of Africans and

Europeans. But there are many Indians, Pakistanis and people of mixed blood in the Federation whose legal status is much closer to that of the African than to the European. Where I speak of discrimination against Africans, therefore, much of what is said, even if no mention is made of the fact, applies equally to Asiastics and other people of colour.

There is also a certain amount of repetition. This is inevitable in describing a situation in which each race reacts and counter-reacts upon the other. The behaviour of the Africans forces a certain attitude upon the European and this new attitude is itself responsible for a further African reaction. Some aspects of every problem are, therefore, common to either race in one form or another and have to be referred to in each case.

Finally, I have been bold enough to suggest a solution. This is something that social scientists are not usually trained to undertake. But most other writers have their solution to the African problem and this book would accordingly be out of step if it did not attempt to sum up what has been said and suggest what might be done. I have not taken very much account of economic or political factors in this proposed solution because I believe that in the last resort the problem is an essentially human one in which we have to recognize that Africans think in many ways differently to ourselves and, most important, that the majority of them are at the present time too embittered to think objectively. They hate the Europeans, not perhaps every European individually but in general because of what has happened to them in the past, and hating them they do not want a fair constitution, partnership, ministerial appointments, higher wages or any of the other sops currently offered to them. They want revenge. Like a man whose house has been burgled, they do not derive great satisfaction if the culprit is caught and punished. They want to be recompensed for the past before they settle down to discuss terms for the future. It is for this reason that when an African leader accepts a new constitution for his people, perhaps one that goes even further in the concessions that it makes than he has ever dreamt possible, this constitution is later refused by his followers. Behaviour of this kind may make the job of constitution-framing incredibly difficult, but it is at least understandable in terms of human nature and it is very understandable indeed in terms of African traditional philosophy. In tribal society the rule was an eye for an eye and if a man murdered another, his first obligation was to make a suitable form of compensation to the family of his victim.

I believe that there is only one way, short of violence, in which the present unhappy scene can be stabilised and inter-racial co-existence achieved. I have set this down briefly in the last chapter.

In conclusion, I should like to express my gratitude to the Beit

Trustees and the Rhodesian Selection Trust for generously enabling me to undertake my studies in Africa. I should also like to express my debt to the writings of the Institute of Race Relations in London and in particular to the work of Philip Mason whose books have been an inspiration both in the depth of their learning and the sympathetic understanding that they bring to the subject.

Contents

	Preface	vii
1	The British Approach	15
2	Early Days in Central Africa	26
3	Culture Shock in Central Africa	43
4	The African at Home	54
5	Bad Citizens	68
6	And Bad Workers	96
7	Today's Masters	114
8	The Advanced Africans	141
9	The End of an Era	162
	Bibliography	175
	Index	177

CHAPTER 1

The British Approach

Referring to India and credited to Queen Victria are the words, 'In their happiness will be our strength, in their contentment our security and in their gratitude our best reward. Liberty will not descend to people. A people must raise themselves up to liberty. It is a blessing which must be earned before it can be enjoyed.'

Therein lay stirring and noble sentiments upon which to build an Empire. As an impetus to Britain's development of backward peoples they echoed all the challenges and the dangers that were to be met. The implications that the Victorians saw were clear. There could be little material reward to those who set themselves the task of bringing civilization to the far corners of the earth. For such a concept to succeed would require men of great personal qualities, backed by imagination, technical skill and vast capital resources.

How far have we measured up to these objectives? It is indeed a hard question to answer objectively, even at the present time. For the story has not run its full course. The task we set ourselves is not everywhere complete. In years to come history will probably place our achievements and rate our successes somewhere in between imperialist exploitation and a genuinely altruistic attempt to develop the backward territories for the benefit of their own peoples.

Today, for reasons that are in part our own fault, the tendency is to lean towards the former view. The world is certainly not yet prepared to acknowldege its debt to those who, in the eighteenth and nineteenth centuries went out to administer, to trade and to spread the Gospel. Grudgingly, perhaps, even now, India will admit that she owes much to Britain for her present position in the world. When Burma and the Sudan come through their present troubles they will both go forward more smoothly and with greater sureness because of the firm foundations laid by British Civil Servants dedicated to the countries they served. Arab historians will one day proclaim the debt they owe to Cromer, to Kitchener, to Milner and to Storrs. On the South American continent, roads, railways, harbours—the whole system of local communications—were pioneered by British engineers and are a lasting monument to their achievements. In China, Malaya, on the islands of the West Indies and Pacific are yet other British-built railways whose connection with this country is remembered perhaps only in the 'Foreign Rails' column of the financial press. Today, few if any of these once proud achievements of British skill are still either owned or even controlled from this country. They have passed into the hands of the people in whose lands they are situated. And it is right that this should happen even if we may sometimes, or on some occasions, regret the manner of their passing.

Commercial considerations apart, the record of these technical achievements is impressive by any standard. No other country has matched it in the past. No single country could produce the capital resources needed for a comparable effort in the second half of the twentieth century.

But what of the builders themselves? The men, often accompanied by their wives, who worked hard and long to create these masterpieces of engineering skill, these States founded on a modern system of administration. They had the technical skill, they usually had the financial resources needed, but did they have the qualities of mind and heart to implement to the full the high hopes of the Queen Empress of India? We in this country believe they had. We have erected statues to their memories and we remember their achievements with pride in our history books. But it is questionable whether this attitude is shared by the rest of the world. Do the people of South American states, of India, Burma, the Arab countries of the Middle East or Malaya feel disposed to erect monuments to their British benefactors? The answer is an emphatic 'No'. If there once were such statues, then these have usually been removed on our departure. In the case of India, Mr Nehru has remarked that any statues of Englishmen in his country that have historic interest will be preserved in museums. The remainder could be disposed of by anybody who wanted them. Sometimes the removal has been carried out with dignity and a measure of respect. In this way the statues of Gordon and Kitchener left Khartoum in the Sudan. In other cases the removal has been more violent. And if there are now other statues in their place, then these are to men who rebelled against the British, not to those who supported them.

This situation has not occurred because those British technicians, explorers, soldiers, traders, pro-consuls—whoever or whatever they might have been—were avaricious, grasping or because they sold their services at too high a price. Undoubtedly there were cases of exploitation, of taking advantage of the local people's lack of commercial acumen. The means we used to acquire and control the Suez Canal can always be held against us, as can commercial exploitation in West Africa, or the conditions laid down for the operation of the South American Railways—to mention but a few of the better-known illustrations. But all the exploitation, all the commercial dishonesty counts as nothing when set against the enormous gain brought by Britain to the territories she called colonial or dependent, or in those countries where she traded the special skills acquired by virtue of her then pre-eminence in the field of industrial engineering.

The British Approach

Commercial faults the local people will forget. Indeed, the majority have long been forgotten. But what they do not forget so easily is our almost uncanny knack of alienating those of them who have striven hardest to emulate us and to raise themselves above the level of their fellows. As Philip Woodruff points out in his second volume of *The Men Who Ruled India* '. . . it is clear that the kind of men England sent to India were throughout successful, indeed movingly successful, with Hos and Sonthals, Nagas and Lushais, and indeed, to a lesser extent, with people everywhere until they were politically awakened. The feeling was mutual; the English liked soldiers, servants, orderlies, tribesmen, the simple people, the people who liked them. Or to put it in another way, they liked those who still accepted the old paternal relationship.'

This failing in India was also our failing elsewhere. Ultimately we were thrown out of the South American states, out of Egypt, Persia and elsewhere for one over-riding reason. We were loathed for our exclusiveness, for our capacity to make the local people feel second-rate in their own lands.

Perhaps these local people were wrong in their judgement. Maybe they saw only one facet of the Englishman, or their judgement had been warped by national politicians or by people bent upon undermining respect for the traditions and ways of life of Britain and the West. But the fact remains that these feelings exist. They are very real and one must attempt to find out why they occur.

The evidence of our exclusiveness and of the bitterness it engendered is not easily found in the history books, or certainly not in the history books published in England. But novels written by people with a special knowledge of the places concerned are an important source of information. Amongst others, the writings of E. M. Forster, Gerald Hanley and Doris Lessing are valuable for their insight into the social behaviour of administrators and settlers in India, Africa and elsewhere. Cumulatively the picture they draw of British behaviour overseas goes far to explain the hostility felt by so many backward peoples for the British living amongst them.

Generalizations are inevitable in dealing with a subject that covers so many lands and so many varying social situations. In India, the Sudan, Burma, and in many of the Colonial territories there was much genuine dedicated service. Generations of men and women gave unsparingly that simple people might prosper and find a greater measure of happiness than they had hitherto known. But how many of those dedicated people are remembered by those whom they served? Are there hundreds, let alone thousands, of British men and women venerated today in countries that have found independence or are fast reaching that goal? Many are, of course, still remembered with affection by simple villagers, peasants and soldiers. But how many can claim still to be remembered with respect or affection by those of their charges who have reached a higher level of education and who have acquired western ways of thinking and behaviour? The answer is singularly few.

Basically the criticism that local people make of the Englishman overseas, whether administrator, soldier, trader, missionary or adventurer is that because of his tendency to exclusiveness he failed to understand or sympathize with the needs and the mentality of those amongst whom he lived or lives and for whose future he made himself responsible. That in spite of his integrity and technological skill, there was a reluctance to associate himself with people differing profoundly in culture and philosophy. A final criticism is that there was a considerable amount of what can only be called individual bad manners.

My own first experience of our exclusiveness came in Egypt. It was during the war and at a time when I was stationed in Cairo. The work I was doing brought me into close contact with Egyptians of all classes and on one occasion a very colourful Sheikh invited me to his home for dinner. Later I returned the compliment. On hearing this, my Colonel, a regular soldier who had spent many years of his service on the Canal, was appalled. 'I cannot understand your wanting to do a thing like that,' he said. 'In my day it could never have happened. We prided ourselves on our exclusiveness.' Needless to say, all Egyptians from the King downwards were 'Wogs' to him, as they were to the majority of British military and civilian personnel in the country.

Egypt, in fact, provides plenty of first hand and indeed contemporary evidence of the attitude and behaviour of British people living in privileged positions in foreign countries. There was, for example, the wartime saying that if a member of the Forces ran over a 'Wog' it was less expensive to the British taxpayer to reverse over him in order to ensure that he died rather than to have to pay compensation for his injuries. The interesting thing about this story is that never in all my time in Egypt did I ever meet anyone who had either reversed over a 'Wog' or indeed knew personally of anybody who had ever done so. What is more important is that I never met an Egyptian who had not heard the story and believed it to be true.

Feelings about facts can be as important as are the facts themselves. It matters little that the story of reversing over 'Wogs' is a complete fabrication, but it matters supremely that Egyptians believe it to be true and quote it as a characteristic piece of British behaviour. Nor does it help the situation to dismiss the whole subject as too contemptible even to discuss seriously. For one thing, such beliefs never occur in isolation. For another, similar ideas are current in other countries and with somewhat more justification.

Yet another and perhaps better known slight to Egyptian pride was

The British Approach 19

the Gezira Club. This is a most beautiful sporting and recreational club situated in an idyllic setting on an island in the Nile in the centre of Cairo. Although technically the constitution of the club allowed Egyptian members, in practice there were never more than a handful who managed to get themselves elected. Until the Egyptians seized foreign property under Colonel Nasser, the club remained a European preserve, set in the most attractive part of the city, a place for all Egyptians to see but for virtually none to enter. India, the Far East, Malaya have all known such clubs. Rarely are local people, even those of Royal blood, permitted to enter. And the existence of such places adds to the undercurrent of resentment.

People may argue that when in a foreign land there is a real need for some place to which an expatriate can go and mix with people of his own race, language group, and way of living. This may be true. But it is equally true that almost whenever this happens, the clannishness of the minority group, particularly if it is in any way also privileged, is resented. An exception to this would seem to be the local Caledonian societies that exist in so many overseas territories. But then perhaps the local people look upon the Scots as a subject race themselves!

Many arguments have been put forward in defence of British exclusiveness abroad, but most of them are at best rationalisations. Certainly, though, in the early days there was little alternative. The various peoples with whom the earliest administrators, traders or military first came in contact were undoubtedly very primitive and their customs struck our ancestors as horribly superstitious and obscene. No doubt very many people would feel much the same today if they found themselves in a comparable situation. In the early days of the nineteenth century, there were no westernised Indians, Sudanese or Africans with whom friendships could easily be formed. The trouble has arisen because the original exclusiveness has persisted long after the time when education and society in India, Africa and elsewhere has rendered it obsolete and calamitous.

In the case of India—and of the Indian Civil Service in particular —it has been suggested that far from being a fault, the aloofness of the average official was in the special circumstances of India, doubly a virtue. It provided not only impartiality, but the ability to disengage. The English could complete their task and go home. Again it has been argued in support of separate clubs and the general tendency to exclusiveness, that only thereby could British standards of integrity and morality be maintained. Victorian morals were, superficially at least, of a high order, and they set a high value on integrity. Arabs, Indians and—in Kipling's words—the 'lesser breeds without the law' revealed very different and, superficially again, much less honourable standards of conduct. To the Victorian Englishman, as to many of his descendants today, the institution of polygamy, the less scrupulous attitude taken towards ownership generally and finance in particular, nepotism, bribery and publicly condoned acts of apparent cruelty, all suggested inferiority. And there was the fear perhaps that living too close to such an overwhelming number of people with lower morals, our own might suffer. Whether it was this fear or not that prompted the Victorians to keep themselves apart, we shall never know. But we do know that this is what they did and we know, too, that they were not particularly careful to keep their own views as to why they did so to themselves.

The second charge levied against the Englishman overseas, and one that sprang directly from his exclusiveness, was that the average administrator, soldier, trader or even missionary, knew next to nothing about the people for whom he was responsible, whom he educated or amongst whom he lived. In his defence it might be said that there was little he could learn before he left home that bore any resemblance to the truth. Most accounts of primitive communities written in the eighteenth and nineteenth centuries, even those compiled by the missionaries, were viciously distorted. The seamy side of life, strange barbaric customs, the natives' apparent stupidity in times of emergency—these were the subjects that caught the early writer's eye, and no tale of foreign parts and of their primitive inhabitants was too fantastic to find ready acceptance.

On arrival in a foreign land there was no incentive for the newcomer to change or modify his pre-conceived impressions of the local people. He found them shunned by his superiors and he soon discovered that it was in his own best interest to do the same. As one by no means unfair critic of the Indian Civil Service put it in 1888 '. . . they seem rather wanting in imagination and sympathy, less inspired by the extraordinary and unprecented phenomena of the country than might have been expected . . . too conventionally English'.[1]

There is a tendency to visualize the Englishman who spends his life overseas as quite a different being to his brother who stays at home. The man overseas is seen by some as a hero, a pioneer, a man devoting his life to the service of dependent peoples. To others this same man is a rogue and often a villain too. Serious literature has been written of both types. Again, the man at home is also seen as a sort of Jekyll and Hyde. Africans and others who have lived under what they call the colonial system profess to find the Englishman in England a liberal and kindly person who is sympathetic to their problems. Yet a cursory reading of the behaviour of the managerial classes in this country up to the time of the second world war gives a different picture.

[1] James Bryce in a letter to his mother.

The British Approach 21

In reality, of course, there are exaggerations on both sides. The Englishman who went overseas and his brother who stayed at home are in fact similar in their thinking and in their behaviour towards their subordinates, whether those subordinates are black, white or brown. The captain of industry at home and the Englishman working overseas were both in their own way and in their own sphere primarily concerned with the achievement of material success. Their pride was that they could create an efficient administrative machine or build a town where before there was desert; that they could divert a river and tame its power to their own uses; that they had built a great factory and then a mansion from its proceeds; that they could sink a shaft far into the bowels of the earth and extract precious minerals therefrom in the face of every kind of natural hazard. These were the challenges they recognized and enjoyed.

None of these people, whether they worked in England or overseas, whether they were engineers, administrators, scientists or doctors, had received any training or been given any guidance in the field of human problems. No attempt was made to suggest that there was as big a challenge in the human material they employed as in the technical objectives they set themselves to master. It is true that the Church has always preached the brotherhood of man. But perhaps this particular approach has not been the right one. Had industrialists, employers, administrators or traders been persuaded that sympathy and understanding of their subordinates' problems was not only good Christianity but also good sound economic common sense, then perhaps they might have been more readily receptive.

Certainly the vast majority of them recognized that they had obligations to their subordinates and obligations that might well transcend the payment of what they regarded, rightly or wrongly, as an honest day's pay for an honest day's work. But they tended to see these extra obligations in purely material terms. The administrator overseas sought to give good plumbing, to eliminate overcrowded houses, to operate railway timetables punctually; the industrialist or commercial man in Britain saw welfare facilities as a means of contracting out of his responsibilities in the field of human relations. The whole approach was well summed up many years ago by a Tanganyika chief who was asked what would be left in Tanganyika if the British left. He answered promptly, 'Footballs'. The philosophy of the Englishmen as administrator or employer in the nineteenth and much of the twentieth centuries has been a contemporary form of bread and circuses, the old Roman medicine for keeping the masses contented.

Unable to provide a system of adequate social security, the Englishman in London or Lahore, Leeds or Lagos has always resorted to charity when sections of the people around him have found themselves in want or difficulty. He distributed food or funds, he worked for the poor, he gave of his time. He did all these things all too often in a way that made him disliked or even hated. He failed to note the warnings of history—warnings that had echoed round the world from the earliest times. 'Why do you dislike me? I have done nothing to help you,' wrote Confucius. Much later Saint Vincent de Paul had warned the Catholic Orders that people were hated for their charity, and nearer to our own day Oscar Wilde wrote, 'Charity, is twice cursed—it hardens him who gives and softens him who takes.' For those who went abroad the lines in Kipling's 'White Man's Burden' were apt and prophetic though sadly unheeded at the time.

> Take up the White man's burden
> And reap his old reward
> The blame of those ye better
> The hate of those ye guard.

The Englishman might have been forgiven his exclusiveness—he might even have been forgiven his ignorance of local custom and local values, because in the last analysis this stemmed from his preference to remain apart. But what he could not be forgiven and what have not been forgotten since are his bad manners. This is a fault that the leaders of a feudal society can never permit themselves. It is, in fact, an axiom of most types of society that one can be rude to equals and it is even quite daring to be rude to superiors; but it is intolerable to be rude to subordinates or inferiors. They cannot hit back at the time. But their memories are long and the means they ultimately have of hitting back are particularly effective. Unfortunately, the Englishman never seems to have mastered this simple fact. And we are still paying the price of this failing, both in our dismal record of industrial relations in Britain as well as in the attitude adopted by most dependent peoples to us overseas.

Obviously there must have been many people who were never knowingly rude. But the behaviour of one or even a few individuals far outweighs their numerical insignificance. As one ex-Colonial Civil Servant and later a Conservative Member of Parliament has written, 'If I had to bequeath my advice to a student of history seeking, ages hence, to understand the decline and fall of the British Empire, I should tell him to read E. M. Forster's *A Passage to India*. That book is a study of the decisive rôle played by individual bad manners in the destiny of princes—and by bad manners I mean an uncharitable failure in human sympathy. Its moral is that every mickle of private insult—much of it almost innocent—by a European man, woman or child to the personality and human dignity of the least important Indian, African or Chinese in the last 200 years has added up to the muckle of anti-Western nationalism with which we find it so hard to cope today. If the individual European in India had had better

The British Approach

manners we should still have a united India, passionately loyal to the Queen-Empress. The same moral should be heeded throughout the dependant territories today.'[1]

When Field Marshal Lord Montgomery visited India in 1960 he found evidence of the same behaviour. In his report in the *Sunday Times* on a conversation with Mr Nehru, he wrote:

> Many visitors came to the house, and the young Nehru listened eagerly to the conversation of his elders, which was generally related to the iniquities of the British Raj and the insulting hehaviour of the English towards Indians. He thus developed early an antipathy towards the alien rulers of his country, although he never seems to have had hostile feelings towards individual Englishmen.'[2]

More will be said of this question of manners when considering the situation in Africa. It is of fundamental importance. Just as the lack of understanding of the people sprung from the Englishman's exclusiveness, so his bad manners sprang from his lack of knowledge. A former Governor of Kenya has remarked, ' "Abroad" has remained to our day, as it has always been for most of the English, a curious place inhabited by "foreigners", who cannot speak English, and who may be talked and joked about in their presence and even pointed at with derision.'[3]

Nor can one leave this question of manners without referring to the rôle of the Englishman's wife. Every allowance must be made for the fact that an Englishwoman in a dependant or backward territory faces very special social difficulties. For one thing, in most of the backward countries the local natives were usually unaccustomed to taking orders from women in their own community and were accordingly reluctant to do so when they first met Europeans. In later years it is a strange but unquestionable fact that many Englishmen serving overseas have, on returning home to find a wife, married beneath them and into a class unused to wielding authority or setting an example. Whatever the reasons may be, the Englishman's wife has received a worse press in the territories in which she lived even than her husband. 'The Englishman is popular wherever he goes until he takes his wife' is one well-known tag East of Suez. Noel Coward put it rather more cruelly in his biography when describing his ENSA performances in India during the war. In this he wrote that he had never realized why the servant population of England had so declined until he went out to India and met the wives of the Englishmen serving or trading there.

The men and women on the spot, the principal actors in the drama,

[1] T. L. Iremonger—*Too Small a Candle*—Corona, July 1957.
[2] *Sunday Times*, 29th July 1961.
[3] Sir Philip Mitchell, G.C.M.G., M.C. Manners. Corona, September 1956.

never really saw the situation as it was or understood the consequences of their behaviour. They did not discern the mounting bitterness, or if they did they generally wrote it off as the result of ill-advised politics advocated by self-seeking and non-representative leaders of the local people. Nor did the average Englishman at home realise what was happneing. He relied upon the man on the spot and on the whole he approved the policies and the actions of his brothers overseas. How could he do otherwise? He had been brought up on stories of native simplicity, backwardness and often ingratitude; on tales of stirring exploits and success achieved in the face of tremendous odds, on tales of benevolent self-sacrifice. These tales, and particularly the repetition of success stories given in the form of lectures, newspaper articles and radio broadcasts were highly dangerous on three counts. They antagonized the native people themselves who knew well enough that their own share in the achievements was rarely given adequate cover. Secondly, they ignored the material and spiritual benefits that we had ourselves received from the incidents concerned. Finally, a public that is fed on such a diet for too long becomes increasingly unable to assess correctly the reasons for reverses or failure when they occur.

Certainly, as successive disasters struck, they took both the people overseas and at home by surprise. Even in the 1920's it would have seemed unthinkable that the British industrial and commercial enterprises in South America were shortly to be expropriated by the local people and the British sent home. In the early 1940's few would have believed that the Egyptians were in a short time to drive us out of the Canal Area, from our bases from Port Said to Suez, and that they would take over our commercial holdings throughout the country. The men on the spot had no inkling early in the 1950's that Moussadeq, the so-despised Persian Prime Minister, would be able to seize Abadan and that in consequence one of our largest and most valuable overseas investments would be lost.

The story unfolds with tragic consistency. Exclusiveness to the point of rudeness, charity distributed in a condescending manner, no social mixing, no delegation of responsibility to local people above a certain minimum level. We paid a high price for keeping Argentinians from the Boards of the local railway companies, for keeping Persians from the Board of the Anglo-Iranian, later the British Petroleum Company with its major holdings in Persia, for electing so very few Egyptians to the Boards of our enterprises in Egypt.

It is a mistake to suppose that we lost the overwhelming proportion of our overseas investments to the Americans to pay for our wartime purchases. By 1939 most of our commercial interests were already virtually lost to us because of our pathetic record in the field of human relations.

The British Approach

One cannot invaldiate this argument by quoting the reception that Republican India accorded the Queen on her 1960 tour, or pointing out that there were 6,000 more Englishmen living and working in India at the time of the visit than there were before independence. The friendships that both Ghana and Nigeria now profess for Britain do not alter the fact that when they were dependent they felt very bitter. Time certainly heals some wounds. A Burmese Civil Servant once remarked to me that now that we have left his country his people remember us only for our integrity and they have forgotten how they hated us for our exclusiveness. Comforting though all this may now be, it will give white settlers in Rhodesia and Kenya little joy to be told that if they are driven out of Africa and their lands confiscated, there is every prospect that their sons may one day return to live as equal partners in the new Africa.

There can be no doubt that the present trend in Central Africa follows the unhappy pattern set in other once colonial or once dependent territories. The white people there show all the familiar traits. There is the old exclusiveness, there is a lack of sympathy for the local people, there are bad manners and there is restrictive legislation.

We may never know in detail why the English in general were so disliked in India at the time of the British Raj, in South America, Burma or elsewhere. The time was too long ago and much of the detail was never recorded. But Central Africa is different. It is barely seventy years since white occupation began. Eye witnesses of early events can be questioned. It is still possible to evaluate the importance of recent history in determining how both European and African behave and how they feel about each other. Some brief historical comment on Central Africa is therefore essential to the proper understanding of European behaviour. This historical introduction is essentially selective. Important events that made little or no mark on European or African attitudes have been omitted. I have given most emphasis to those situations that have tended to develop the character or personality of either race and I have also included incidents that though trivial in themselves have nonetheless cumulatively left their mark on race relations.

CHAPTER 2

Early Days in Central Africa

Exploration of Central Africa began in earnest in the early 1890's. And in the course of the ensuing seventy odd years there has been a breathtaking expansion of towns, factories and mines. Roads, bridges, railways and air ports have created a vast communications network. Money has been spent lavishly. The schools, hospitals and the University are all amongst the most modern in Africa and Africans have benefited considerably from these developments. They have been given free schooling, hospitalization, a variety of social amenities in the towns and a great deal has been done to improve farming methods in the tribal areas. Yet the whole fabric of the territory is rocked today by the bitterness of its native inhabitants for the white people who have made their homes there and done so much to create a modern thriving economy.

This bitterness may be due in part to the existence of the same British characteristics that were discussed in the previous chapter. But in Central Africa there are two additional special circumstances that have created a profound influence on the situation. The first of these is that though the original idea for the exploration of the area was British, the whole expedition was planned and mounted in South Africa. The second circumstance is that, in the case of Southern Rhodesia, there was no question of developing the country for the benefit of its African inhabitants. Rhodes and his colleagues intended to create a territory on the lines of the Union of South Africa. It was to be a white man's country and the white men were quite prepared to annex it by force if force was necessary. As it turned out, force was necessary. Southern Rhodesia was taken by the sword and no promises were made to the African inhabitants that there would ever be self-government for them nor any of the other benefits that Africans elsewhere had come to expect from Britain.

In the case of the South African origin of the expedition there is much that is complex and paradoxical. The British and the Boers who together made up the first pioneer column to enter Rhodesia had much in common in their attitude towards Africans. The reason for this common approach has to be sought in their respective histories, histories that though very diverse in origin were yet to lead to a strange similarity of outlook.

The Boers were descended from seventeenth century Calvinistic stock, one of the most puritanical of the Christian sects. Their outlook on life was of necessity a narrow one, for their only reading was the

Early Days in Central Africa 27

Bible. Their law was that of the Old Testament, every word of which they believed to have been divinely dictated. Yet they were also a people of many fine qualities, not least of which was the importance they attached to honour and to hospitality.

Following the British occupation of the Cape early in the nineteenth century the majority of the Boers set off towards the North, into the then unknown, to found a new home that would be free from the taint of the ungodly living that they associated with all those who did not live and think as they. On this Great Trek, as it was named, they fought a series of running battles with bands of pastoral Africans at that time moving down towards the South of the Continent. In these battles the Boers were sometimes victorious and sometimes they were defeated. But in the manner of their living they fought fairly though ferociously, and on balance European firearms proved too much for primitive bravery armed only with the spear and the bow. Viewed from afar these defeats of the African must seem brutal and even barbaric. Yet when the Boers were fighting Africans as man to man far more vicious methods of slaying indigenous people were being used elsewhere. America and possibly Australia exist in their present form today because of the absolutely ruthless and almost complete extermination of the aboriginal inhabitants of these territories. Had the Boers applied in South Africa the methods used by the early colonists in North America, their title to permanent possession of South Africa would be as valid today as the Americans own.

In moments of danger or disaster the Boers drew great moral comfort from the belief that they were under the especial care of Providence. God, they believed, was guiding them, as long before he had guided the Israelites, to a promised land. They felt themselves to be a chosen people, and set aside in particular from the heathen black, the children of Ham, by whom they were surrounded. Although their attitude was and still is very much that of Herrenvolk, nonetheless, they treated black men fairly and firmly, both in war and whenever they had dealings with them.

Though the liberal attitude towards Africans that is found in the Cape province was inspired largely by Britain, it is a sad commentary on human nature that the discriminatory legislation that was later to develop in the mining, commercial and urban areas of the Transvaal, Orange Free State and Natal were also British inspired. The Boers had virtually no part in the early discovery and exploitation of gold and diamonds that together were to turn the Union of South Africa so quickly from a relatively poor agricultural country to one in which the standard of living of its white people was amongst the highest in the world. The mines of Kimberly and Johannesburg were developed for the greater part by British capital and by British technicians. Great fortunes were made, great towns and later great industries grew up based upon the country's golden economy. And the people who built these towns and sunk these mines, the early British settlers, proceeded from the start to safeguard themselves and their descendants against either direct African competition in the economic field or African intrusion into their social lives. This they achieved largely by legislative action. They laid down what jobs an African might do and those which he might not. Herein lay the origins of the economic colour bar. Other legislation restricted where Africans might live, the rights they might enjoy in those areas where they did live, who they could or could not marry and how far they might join together in order to press for better conditions of living or working.

From these two very different approaches sprang the respective attitudes of British and Boer to African natives. The Boers believed in a divine right to occupy Southern Africa—and in their minds God had not drawn the boundary line at the Limpopo—and they believed just as firmly that Providence had intended the African to occupy a lower status than the white man. One can decry this attitude and even ridicule it. But then most people's spiritual beliefs and illogical superstitions can be treated in like manner by unbelievers. Few if any of a people's spiritual beliefs are open to exact proof and the Boers are, in any case, not the only people who believe themselves to be a chosen people to whom God had given a Promised Land. The Boer never liked the British occupying the same territory as himself but on balance he saw them as less of a threat to his security than the African. He reckoned that in time he would get the better of them as indeed ideologically he did.

The British on the other hand feared the African as constituting a threat to his economic survival. They had built up for themselves a standard of living that had few parallels. And the greatest threat to this standard of living was the African. So, as far as legislation could control the situation, they resorted to legislation. Both groups of Europeans then, for their respective reasons, feared to allow the African scope for advancement. Their common fears brought the two communities together in a way that would never otherwise have been possible. Though there might be little difference in practice between the two attitudes, nonetheless, the Africans quickly made a distinction. He recognized that Boer and British attitude differed in spirit. As he saw it the Boer philosophy could be summed up in the words 'Bless you my servant' and the British as 'Curse you my brother'. All the evidence suggests that of the two he prefers the former.

From such basically different but in practice similar points of view sprang the Rhodesian way of life.

The second conditioning factor in the attitude and behaviour of the Rhodesian settlers derived from the purpose of the initial ex-

Early Days in Central Africa   29

ploration. The early pioneer carried up no lofty idealistic concept of raising the humble African to find a new horizon, or indeed of schooling him for self Government. The justification for the exploration was a permit to 'dig in one hole' given to them under some degree of pressure by Lobengula, King of the Matabele. Few of those who made up the first party to enter what was to become Southern Rhodesia had any illusion as to the real nature of their enterprise or that the concession they had gained from the king were little more than a fiction designed to keep both the Matabele and the people at home ignorant of their true intentions. They entered the country as gold prospectors. They took with them what Lobengula himself noted was an inordinately large body of police. Within a few years they had established themselves, defeated the Matabele in two wars and founded a new European territory in Africa. Expansion in those early days was, however, seriously limited to the resources available and to a lesser extent by public opinion in Britain. Had Rhodes possessed more men and been given more encouragement by the British Government, he would have acquired an outlet to the sea through Portuguese East Africa and the territories to the north of the Zambesi, Northern Rhodesia and Nyasaland that were ultimately secured by Treaty to Britain, would have been taken by force as was the case of Southern Rhodesia. Had that occurred there would have been no Colonial Office responsibility for the areas and many of the difficulties of the present time that spring from Northern Rhodesia and Nyasaland being administered by Britain and Southern Rhodesia being largely independent would never have occurred.

Those who made up the initial pioneer column into Rhodesia were a picked bunch. They had to be strong and active, young but not raw, and within the age group 25-35. They represented a cross-section of all the trades and backgrounds that would be necessary in opening up a new country. All had some experience of life in South Africa where the majority had lived either on Boer farms or in the British mining areas. Each of the young men selected and the 500 police who constituted their escort were promised a farm of 3,000 acres that they were expected to be able to work and, if necessary, defend.

The story of how the Matabele were tricked into permitting this large force, ostensibly of miners, into their country need not now be repeated. One day, perhaps, an African nationalist movement may find cause to resurrect it with such trimmings as may be necessary to win popular votes or else support for a policy of violence. It certainly was not one of Britain's most honourable of arrangements. But it enabled the white men to gain a foothold in the counrty from which they never retreated. Two armed attempts by the Matabele in 1893 and 1896 failed to eject them. Thereafter the African south of the

Zambesi was pacified and the European settled down and established a way of life that was to some extent similar to that of South Africa although, because no particularly rich gold deposits were found, on a somewhat more modest scale. But the link with South Africa remained a strong one both personally and ideologically to the extent that a referendum held in 1922 to decide whether Southern Rhodesia should go into the Union was only defeated by 8,744 votes to 5,989. The deciding factor in the decision was said to have been the lower tax structure ruling in Rhodesia.

From the earliest days of their arrival, the pioneers sought the help of the local Africans in the construction of their homes, in the operation of their townships, mining and farming activities, in the build-up of what was to become the Rhodesian way of life. Few of the Africans spoke either English or Afrikaans and thus could only be employed in unskilled and usually menial tasks. In those days, therefore, and indeed for many a long year thereafter the European never imagined that their position *vis-a-vis* the African could markedly change. The legislation they introduced mirrored this view. Based on the South African pattern it assumed a permanently rural African who left his tribal home from time to time to seek European employment, but who returned thereafter to his permanent home amongst his own people in what were early designated as African Reserves.

The Municipal Act of 1897 gave municipalities the power to discriminate against Africans in their bye-laws. The permitted discrimination included the control and regulation of African housing, when and where Africans could be at various hours of the day and night, and the allocation of separate buses and other facilities for Africans. These powers gave the municipal authorities almost unlimited freedom in the conditions they imposed on Africans coming into the towns to work. And in certain cases they took full advantage of these facilities. Thus, in 1906 under Notice 66 it was laid down in Bulawayo that no native could use any side-walk within the municipality and should he be convicted of such an offence a fine of up to £2 could be imposed.

Such legislation played an important part in shaping the pattern of race relations generally and African advancement in particular. The existence of the powers granted to the Europeans was in itself a cause of resentment and though there was, for example, no conviction of an African for being on the side-walk until 1934—and then it was set aside on the grounds that if an African was permitted to enter a shop then he must be expected to use the side-walk—the existence of the legislation, the permanent threat that it implied and the attitude of superiority it created in the Eureopeans, all contrived together to increase the bitter feeling that started to grow amongst the town Africans from the earliest days.

Early Days in Central Africa

The bedrock of the whole legislative system was, however, the Land Apportionment Act that some Europeans have termed their Magna Charta. This Act laid down areas for African and for European occupation and thereby made it unnecessary for Southern Rhodesia to prohibit by law the marriage of European and African. The Act effectively prevented this by making it virtually impossible for the two races ever to be able to live together.[1] Other legislation was designed to promote the security of the European. Thus Africans were limited to certain unskilled occupations, they were called upon to carry passes in the urban areas, to be medically examined at set periods and to vacate their homes if they were not gainfully employed. Certain legislation was also passed that though it might be classified as discriminatory, was nonetheless of some value to the African and the times. This was principally operative where commercial dealings between Africans and Europeans, particularly over land, could lead to the African being exploited.

Traditionally the Englishman has shown himself the friend of the simple peasant, the unspoilt savage, the wild, untamed inhabitant of desert and forest areas. It was so in India and elsewhere. The Englishman has got along with these people well enough until they began to copy his ways and seek a basis of equality. In Rhodesia this was never really the case. Apart from Cecil Rhodes who won a great measure of personal respect from the Africans with whom he dealt, the early settlers treated the simple, unsophisticated Africans with scant respect or courtesy. These Europeans had, after all, been selected for their brawn and capacity to surmount the physical hardships of a rugged life rather than for any qualities of integrity or the ability to handle subordinates, particularly backward ones, fairly and effectively. Thus the story is current in Southern Rhodesia today of how in the early days of the occupation a pleasant enough way of spending a Saturday afternoon was to sit on one's stoop (porch) taking pot-shots with a rifle at passing Africans. If one was bagged, it was only necessary to fill up a form and hand it to the local Native Commissioner. Like the story of reversing over Wogs in Egypt, I never met anybody who had either shot an African in this way or who had actually known personally of it being done. But I met many Africans as well as Europeans who believed that such shootings had occurred. The story accords in any case with the many acts of cruelty, discourtesy and rudeness that can be more authoritively vouched for. One well-known story is told by Rhodes himself. When he took the uncannily brave and brilliant step of going unarmed and alone into the Motopos Hills to parley with the Matabele Chiefs after the

---

[1] It is pertinent to mention that the first Mixed Marriages Act passed in Africa was introduced by the British in Natal in 1897 to forbid the marriage of Europeans with Indians.

second rebellion had been crushed, one of the Chiefs told how he had gone down into Bulawayo to pay his respects to the Chief Magistrate. Having made his presence known to the great man he was kept waiting all day. Towards evening he sent a second polite message to the effect that though he did not wish to hurry the Chief Magistrate, neither he nor his elders who accompanied him had eaten all day and they were hungry. He further pointed out in his message that when a white man visited his kraal, a beast was always killed and provided for the guests. The Chief did not have long to wait for the answer. It was to the effect that there were stray dogs in the town and he might kill one of these for his meal. Whether the reply was sent by the Magistrate himself or by one of his subordinates is immaterial. If by the former, then such behaviour is inexcusable. If it was sent by a subordinate, it must have had the tacit approval of the Magistrate for it would not have been sent to a man he was known to respect.

The history books do not, as a rule, tell of the callous attitude shown by many of the early settlers in their dealings with Africans. Several instances that rival anything that happened in South Africa have been quoted by Philip Mason.[1] There is, for example, the case of the party of soldiers engaged on building a fort. 'Till the fort was built, they believed they were in danger; an escort of forty-three armed men had been attacked not three miles away in the last two days and there had been fires in the hills all round every night, presumed to belong to hostile forces. A patrol saw a native woman with a child near the camp and caught her, though she tried to run away. Questioned, she said there were no natives in the neighbourhood, an obvious lie; she also said she was going to a chief whose kraal was in the opposite direction from that she was taking when caught. She was judged, on the ground of these two statements, to be a spy. "There was no means of keeping her in safe keeping, escort could not be spared to take her to Gwelo; if released, enemy would have at once full information of weakness of force. After full consideration Board of Officers condemned her to death." In a later and fuller report, the story continues : "In order to have the sentence carried out in the most humane manner, I told the adjutant to have her taken out of camp by colonial boys without being told the decision and to send the orderly non-commissioned officer to see this order carried out without her knowing anything about it. . . . As regards the child, it was only after the return to camp of the escort that I learnt, on asking where it was, that it had been shot." The High Commissioner reported to the Colonial Office that "the proceedings indicate a disregard for human life . . . and were irregular to an extent which amounted to a parody of justice" but "in view of the wide discretion granted by military rule and custom to officers commanding isolated

[1] Philip Mason. *The Birth of a Dilemma.* O.U.P. 1958.

detachments" he was not prepared to say a crime had been committed and considered that "grave animadversion" and "a severe reprimand" would meet the case.

'This was an exception; it would not otherwise have come to the notice of the Colonial Office. But it has been dwelt on because it is an example of mixed standards and ideas. That a peasant woman captured by armed men of another race and of an utterly alien culture should blurt out that none of her own people were near, that she should give an unsatisfactory account of her movements, was not really surprising; to regard this as evidence that she was a spy was to judge her as a rational creature capable of considering the effect of her answers. But in deciding on the sentence of death, the court was influenced largely by the inconvenience of disposing of her in any other way; in deciding not to inform her of the sentence, they had clearly ceased to think of her as the prisoner of a court-martial capable of defence, still less as a human soul able to communicate with a Deity; they thought of her rather as a cow which should not see the butcher before he struck. And as for the child—no doubt everyone on the Board of Officers had been shocked by what he heard of what the Matabele did to the children of the Mashona. But this child, like its mother, had not really been thought of as a human being.'[1]

It is quite evident that the rough and ready justice of these early settlers was so rough and ready as to be barely justice at all. There was, for example, the Battlefields case. This concerns money stolen from a visitor to the Battlefields Mine in 1911. 'The manager said he would find out who had done it. There had been other thefts in the district and, he said, an attempt at rape; he was determined to get to the bottom of the thefts. Three "boys" in the compound were suspected; they would not confess so were tied up and flogged till they fainted. They were tied up for the night and were flogged again, making in all three successive days; two of them, Mangesi and Sixpence, died, one of them on the day after the third flogging. The immediate cause of death was pneumonia in one case, pleurisy and pneumonia in the other; exposure and chill following shock were said in the medical evidence to be likely to cause pneumonia. The accused —Macaulay, Fraser, Murray, and McBryde—were charged with culpable homicide, not murder, as it was not alleged that they had intended to cause death—though they might well have been expected to know that death was likely to result. Their plea that they were all under the influence of one MacArthur can hardly be taken seriously; still less another plea that the three natives had flogged each other. No verbatim report of his summing-up is in existence, and *The Rhodesia Herald's* report must obviously contain gaps; in this report, the judge leaves it open to the jury to decide whether the accused

[1] *Op cit* pp. 207 et seq.

OMS—C

were so much under MacArthur's influence as not to be responsible for their actions but he must surely be assumed to have told them something of the law. Even orders given to a person under military discipline do not constitute a defence for an act in itself illegal. He did, even in the report, make it clear that "provocation" applies only to an act done "in hot blood", and with ironic understatement he left it to them to decide whether such unbearable provocation could be supposed to last three days. The only plea the accused can really have had any belief in was that, since there were no police in the area, it was their duty to keep order. But they could hardly have pleaded that as self-appointed police they were entitled to use torture to extract confessions. It took the jury only ten minutes to reach a verdict of not guilty on all counts.'[1]

Another example of the same approach to maintaining law and order, was the case of an African charged with attempted rape. Had the case occurred in a counrty in which no legal distinction existed between different classes of citizens, it is probable that the charge would have been entered as a simple case of assault. 'The complainant went out for a walk between four and five in the afternoon; she passed a native as she walked; a little later she was attacked, she believed by the same native; she struggled with him "for twenty minutes" and eventually gave him a blow in the face, at which he ran away bleeding profusely from the nose. She later identified a man, changed her mind, identified another, changed her mind again, picked the accused (Dumba alias Sixpence) from a parade of nine. This was shaky enough; in most courts, identification would be vitiated by the two previous mistakes. But to add to the uncertainty, Dumba's employer, whose word as a white man was unimpeachable, said that at five o'clock Dumba was milking peacefully and showed no signs of bleeding or anything else unusual. Dumba was found guilty by a majority of seven to two and sentenced to six years hard labour and twenty-five lashes. Did he get the benefit of any reasonable doubt?

'The Rhodesians wished to do justice. But in their approach to justice they were necessarily governed by their basic assumptions, high among which came a fixed mental picture of "the African" as lustful and violent, only to be kept in place with a stern hand. And to that picture went an unspoken, unformulated, perhaps unconscious, feeling that when a native has committed a crime, a native ought to be punished; one should try of course to punish the right man, but if by any chance it should be the wrong man, well, punishment would still serve to discourage the others. Perhaps no one would have put that feeling into words; perhaps it did not exist; if not, it

[1] Op. cit. pp. 300-301.

must at least have seemed as though it existed to Dumba and his friends.'[1]

It is hardly surprising that the High Commissioner of South Africa at the time, Lord Milner, once remarked 'The treatment of the blacks has been scandalous'.

Though few of these instances of gross inhumanity are remembered by the Africans today in any detail, the attitude the incidents created in the minds of the Africans in those far off days has been passed down to their children in a vague form of anti-white distrust and bitterness. African children, in fact, have no need to have chapter and verse for their parents' attitude, they see sufficient situations of a like nature in their own lifetime to justify the resentment they know their parents felt, as well as to create their own at first hand.

Following the Matabele wars in Southern Rhodesia and the signing of treaties with the Chiefs of Northern Rhodesia and Nyasaland, the three territories settled down to a long period of tranquillity in so far as relations between black and white were concerned. There were other problems to occupy fully the time and initiative of the white settlers. Farming was not easy—rainfalls were spasmodic and unpredictable and many little known diseases broke out to make the rearing of cattle, or the growing of crops, a most hazardous affair. Those who took up mining found little that was comparable to the Gold Reef in South Africa and though other mineral deposits were available they were seldom easily worked.

Year after year the stream of Africans moving from the rural areas to the towns grew in proportion. In the early days they came in to work for very short periods. But as the years passed, more and more of them cut adrift from their homes in the reserves and attempted to settle down in the precarious conditions of the growing African townships that sprawled outside most of the European urban centres. The Africans took jobs as domestic servants, as waiters or cleaners in hotels, or as unskilled workers in mines and factories. They came initially, to earn money to pay the poll tax imposed upon them by the Government. But, once they had visited the urban areas they came again, drawn by a variety of factors. Some came because they found tribal discipline harsh after living away from it. Some came out of curiosity to see the white man's world. Others came to save up money to buy a wife, or to gain prestige for having made a long journey. Many who came never returned home. Some of these brought their wives with them but the majority relied on the presence of the few but readily available local women from which to take a wife or a temporary companion.

Within the urban areas set aside for their own occupation the

[1] *Op. cit.* pp. 310-311.

Africans were left very much to their own devices. Sometimes they were permitted to build their own homes, but, more usually, they had to find shelter in some form of municipal or mine accommodation provided for them. One scans municipal records of the early years in vain for reference to African affairs. In so far as such references were made, they concerned the provision of sanitary buckets and incinerators, and the impression is given that the fly was a far greater problem than the African. The social problems building up in a community composed largely of single men, the dangers to health and mind of unhealthy overcrowded homes—none of these things gave any cause for anxiety.

The European settlers experienced their first major check in the early 1930's. Two things then happened in quick succession to show that however resourceful they might be, however great their courage or their skill, yet there were forces in the world outside that could halt or seriously retard their progress. The first check came when Lord Passfield reaffirmed the Devonshire Declaration on African paramountcy. Settlers in Northern Rhodesia and Nyasaland were greatly alarmed. Those in Southern Rhodesia feared that if the British Government was going to favour Africans in the two northern territories it might well take the same line in the south. Subsequent statements in the Declaration that other races would receive 'equal treatment in accordance with their several needs' did not allay these fears for it was clearly recognized that whatever else might or might not happen, the Document was going to be of great propaganda value to African nationalists.

Hard on the heels of this blow came the economic recession that was to reaffirm the settlers' ultimate dependence upon the world outside. The slump years, indeed, hit them badly. Many hundreds of Europeans in Southern Rhodesia worked for their keep and 1s. a day.[1] In Northern Rhodesia the situation for many Europeans became so serious that hundreds of them had to be given food by District Commissioners.

As the 1930's progressed, forces began to build up that, had they been heeded, many of the difficulties now besetting the politicians in England and Rhodesia could have been avoided. In a word, the trouble was detribalization. This was something for which the European settlers had never bargained. Their policy, if the very *laissez-faire* attitude they had adopted towards Africans entering the towns could

---

[1] Though they may not have recognized it at the time, the work they did was a remarkably fine investment for the country. They laid two concrete strips the width of motor car wheels apart, along most of the major highways. Before this was done the roads were mostly sand or dust tracks and were frequently unpassable. The strips gave the Colony twenty years of what was, for Africa, better than average motoring.

be called a policy at all, was that the African would remain a countryman who came to work in town or mine from time to time to seek temporary employment. What he did in his spare time while he remained in town did not greatly concern them. It was felt that the legislation, almost entirely copied from South Africa, would keep him in his place, but, when he was not gainfully employed, or when he was too old to work any more, his real home was considered to be the tribal reserves.

Unfortunately, things did not work out in this convenient way. Though there was little or no work for women, they could earn ready money from the many men living cooped-up unnatural lives in the shanties or location houses. Inevitably children were born and there gradually grew up a community of young African men and women who did not have a reserve home to which they could return when unemployed. Few of these young people knew their father and they lacked the discipline and respect for authority that tribal life would have given them. The most formative period of their lives was spent in the company of large numbers of itinerant men and in a community with no social values, no public opinion, no loyalties and in an environment of poverty, vice and most of the social diseases that boded nothing but ill for a future in which they would one day come to take a part.

The first warnings that the long period of tranquillity was at an end came in 1935 with African strikes and riots at Nkana in Northern Rhodesia. Bloodshed and gunfire put an end to the disturbances, but, for the first time in their lives, the Europeans had it driven home to them in the most telling manner, that they were living in a territory in which the numerically superior Africans were at last beginning to bestir themselves. The Nkana incident gave African leadership its first chance to show itself. What this leadership may or may not have learnt from its first attempt at revolution does not matter. The Europeans, for their part, were shocked to learn that the majority of African trouble-makers could not be sent back to tribal homes for they had been born and bred in the town itself. And there were other lessons to be learned too. The European miners and settlers noted how throughout the strike and during the incidents that followed it, the Police and the Administration had seemed to be on the African side. For the European Mineworkers Union there was an even more startling discovery. Henceforth, management was not their only adversary. There was going to be difficulty with the Africans as well.

Strikes and attempts to organize were not the only clouds on the horizon. The social situation in the urban areas in which the detribalized Africans were living was beginning to get out of hand. By 1938 the incidence of venereal diseases in the towns was reaching staggering proportions. Venereal disease is in some ways a very fair barometer of social distress and the Medical Officer in Bulawayo wrote to the Mayor of the town in the following words : 'The magnitude of the problem becomes more and more apparent and it becomes increasingly evident that unless native social conditions be radically altered, our treatment campaigns are not going to be rewarded with the full measure of success which the not inconsiderable expenditure should be capable of giving to us.' He went on to stress the dangers of an unbalanced population which the development of industry, with its demand for male workers, was tending to bring about.

These and other warnings passed unheeded. The Africans would have had to show a united front for anything to be done and this they were not then in a position to do. On the whole they were still content to accept shockingly low standards of accommodation in exchange for the white man's money, whilst tribal custom was still strongly enough respected for a man to obtain help from a relative should he be in need. The traditional African social system was in those days still in a position to underwrite the low wages and scanty accommodation provided by the municipalities or European employers. All this was well enough known to the Europeans who felt that in the last resort they always had their legislation and this they felt was capable of holding in check any attempt the Africans might make to create a powerful opposition.

African affairs were still not taken very seriously. Certainly not as seriously as the question of finding ways and means of developing the industrial potential of the country. Just prior to the war all other issues were forced into the background and a typical illustration of this trend is shown in the report of one of the municipal authorities. 'The general conditions of the natives in the location, both social and economic, have been catered for by the erection of large extensions to the beer hall.'

Europan settlers cannot easily avoid the charge that in these largely trouble-free days before the war they were singularly insensitive to the social problem—and indeed to the political problems—that they were building up for themselves. Looking back, it is easy enough, perhaps, to see this. In their defence it could be suggested that they were living at a time when it was still possible for General Smuts to mow down Africans with machine-guns in South Africa without the conscience of the world being unduly troubled. Twenty years were in fact to pass before a similar incident, this time at Sharpville, was to create so wide a measure of international disapproval.

The war years brought immense economic benefits to each of the territories. The demand for copper for strategic purposes called for as rapid an increase as possible in the output of the Northern Rhodesian mines. Secondary industry in Southern Rhodesia received a similar boost and Nyasaland, traditionally the supplier of labour for these two territories, was able to send even more of its men away to earn and remit monies home. In Southern Rhodesia permits to build factories were issued with little or no heed to the availability or otherwise of African housing. Squatters' camps grew up on every side, as a spirit of 'get-rich-quick' motivated both Europeans and Africans. The Europeans saw ready markets for whatever they could produce and an almost inexhaustible supply of unskilled African labour that seemed to accept pitifully low standards of accommodation if cash wages were forthcoming.

There was more to come out of the war for the Rhodesians, however, than economic benefits. After the dust and havoc of battle had cleared, there rose from the ashes a host of new philosophies that called for social justice for all, for an end of racial prejudice and underprivilege. Inevitably a world pledged to such principles turned its eyes to those countries in which inequality in one form or another was known to exist. The United Nations Organization in particular, through its special agencies, existed to publicize such cases and to call upon the free world to eradicate them. Rhodesia could not escape this critical survey.

The Africans sensed these changes and it gave them a new confidence and a new purpose. Yet there was much organization to be done before they could hope to rally outside liberal forces to their aid. The legislation in Southern Rhodesia that barred them from forming trade unions was one handicap. The problems of organizing largely migrant labour was a second.

The Europeans did not see these changes so clearly. They were aware of an increasingly hostile world press and the criticism by people whom they felt did not understand the African, caused them considerable annoyance. But they did not take such criticisms very seriously, for by then they were too busy exploiting the sellers' market that existed all over Africa in the post-war years for goods and services. The position and the rights of the African would have to wait their turn. The priority was not high.

The post-war industrial development was largely undertaken by a new type of immigrant, men who left England in their thousands at the end of hostilities, many of them to escape from the implementation of socialist theories, the welfare state, the increasingly powerful trade union movement and the heavy incidence of taxation. They were already favourably disposed to the kind of social situation that existed in Rhodesia before they arrived. They found no appeal in the traditions of the country over which they spread their bricks, mortar and cement. Whereas before the war every man and boy, woman and child knew of and recalled with pride the exploits of their parents at the time of the Matabele wars, the new post-war immigrant leaders and those who came to work for them had no idea what the Matabele wars were about, when they had taken place, and they felt no inclination to find out. They took the African situation as they found it. They saw large numbers of disorganized, ill-paid and unskilled labour that took what was offered avidly, gave a most indifferent day's work for equally indifferent pay and that had no means of enforcing any improvement in the conditions offered. Few of these new Rhodesians troubled to look any further. The situation, in fact, was the same as before the war, only rather more so. There were more locations, more beer halls, more overcrowded houses but no more rights. Indeed discriminatory legislation was stepped up with a new Urban Areas and Accommodation Act that increased both the number of passes to be carried and the restrictions of movement upon the Africans themselves.

The only people within the territories who actually saw the dangers towards which the Europeans were heading, were the Health Departments. To them the mounting toll of disease, overcrowded homes and malnutrition spelt dangers in plenty in the near future. Their warnings were clear enough but they too still went unheeded. The Medical Officer of Health for Bulawayo, perhaps the worst of the urban areas from the point of view of overcrowding, had this to say in his report to the Council for 1947. 'The celibate and unhomely existence imposed by residence in communal hutments appeals to the native as little as it would to Europeans and those who have set up house with their wives and families in shanties constructed of petrol tins and sacking, their neighbours an unwilling source of water and the whole world their latrine, are not likely to be willing to change their style for the monastic seclusion of the camps (built by the Council for Migrant Labour). It is perfectly true that a given area can be cleared up if attention is concentrated upon it, but the trouble will certainly break out somewhere else; the position must be accepted that human beings, whatever their colour may be, cannot with any success be directed along paths which are at variance with those indicated by nature, and the only hope of finding a satisfactory solution is to provide accommodation of which the natives will willingly avail themselves.'

A situation of this nature could not long continue in the post-war world. If warnings from within the territories could be ignored, the European settlers were forced more and more to recognize the force of overseas criticism. The suppression of trade union activities in Southern Rhodesia, the stalling on African advancement on the copper mines in the north, the various pass laws and other discriminatory legislation, together with increasingly frequent instances of inexcusably bad behaviour to individual Africans living in the territories and to coloured visitors, often of diplomatic status, all surprised and shocked even those in Britain who claimed to champion the cause of the European settlers. There was ammunition in plenty for vocal left-wing organizations, while liberals everywhere were quick to criticize and scold.

Yet the settlers, particularly the post-war variety, were in all essential respects the same kind of people as those who had remained at home. They had the same social background, had received the same liberal education and they had the same religious beliefs. Here perhaps is the clue to the situation. The settlers were not themselves responsible for what was happening.

To live in Africa is to be subject to a variety of little understood and, as yet, scarcely studied social pressures and tensions. The racial attitudes that appear to many psychologists as the basic cause of the inability of white people to mix freely with coloured people are believed to spring from the European's horror of racial mixture. There is certainly an almost morbid fear of miscegenation pervading every settler's thinking on the subject of race. In part this springs from the respective ideology of Briton and Boer. The oft-quoted question 'do you want . . .' implies that daughter, sister, mother would, if there was free choice. Both elements of the early settler population were determined that there should be no such opportunity. And each had their own reasons for taking this line. The Victorian Englishmen had made an ideal of chivalry and he tended to set the women of his own race on a pedestal apart from the masculine brutality he recognized in himself. The Boer element had behind them long generations of conscious endeavour to preserve racial purity on grounds of religion, if nothing else.

But, as Professor MacCrone comments : 'This obsession with race purity is, of course, so much rationalizing, since its real aim is to keep sexuality in the form of a potential superior sexual rival at bay. The idea of a white woman in the arms of a black man, especially if she is there of her own free will, is enough to give rise to the most pronounced reactions in the white man.'[1]

There is, of course, nowhere near the same horror of white men taking coloured women and when Rhodesians are asked why, if there is such a strong aversion to mixing the races, this freedom for the men is tolerated and not forbidden in law, as is the union of coloured men with white women, the reply is often rather naïvely to the effect that to legislate in this way against men is still too close to Mr Rhodes's day. The implication that the great man had such weaknesses himself is less significant in any consideration of the extent of the hostility to miscegenation than is the fact that there are today in the Rhodesias some 20,000 people of mixed blood.

Fears of racial mixture are there, and are real enough, but it is too

[1] MacCrone, I. D. *Race Attitudes in South Africa.* Witwatersrand University Press. 1937.

facile to attempt to blame all Europeans' behaviour on these emotions. For one thing, Englishmen have shown the same attitude to dependant white communities as they reveal to black Africans. The more significant reasons for their behaviour are two-fold. In the first place there is a factor that has been called 'Culture Shock'. And the second reason lies in the behaviour and attitude of the Africans themselves. Both of these two factors must be considered in some detail if the overall situation is to be understood and proper remedies found.

CHAPTER 3

Culture Shock in Central Africa

Relations between individuals, however close, are seldom harmonious for long. How much more likely then that groups of people with different social backgrounds and different political ambitions should disagree amongst each other strongly. This is particularly the case where people make new homes for themselves in countries with a different level of civilization to their own. In cases of this kind, and Central Africa provides a classic example, the newcomer as well as the native peoples, are subject to a variety of little understood stresses and tensions.

It is easy but dangerous to minimize the frustration and the resulting hostility that develops when people are called upon to adjust their usual mode of living to that of an alien group or even to put up with that same alien group's social behaviour at close quarters. It is true that we are all of us at all times making minor adjustments to those around us. In contemporary English society we are constantly having to adjust to peoples of different economic or social classes to ourselves, to people from different geographical areas, people of different age groups, different occupations or faiths, even to people of different racial groups. Generally these adjustments cause us few problems. This is largely because in the last resort we have the advantage of sharing a common language, we have common institutions, a law we both accept and understand and a commonly approved system of conduct. In a word, we share a common culture. But, when people do not share common institutions, language or have a commonly approved system of behaviour, when the culture is different, then adjustment to these other people becomes more difficult in proportion to the extent that they are different in their behaviour.

It is important to recognize in the context of race relations how vital is the question of cultural differences.

Culture has unfortunately come to mean something very different to what in fact it really is. To many it is equated with a learned or even highbrow range of activities usually associated with the arts. Nobody would deny Beethoven and Shakespeare form part of the inheritance of western culture or even, perhaps, that cricket is an essential feature of British culture. But these are only activities on the fringes of our culture. An Englishman or a German can remain English or German and be seen to be such when neither has the slightest familiarity with Beethoven, Shakespeare or cricket. The things that really characterize us as English or German are far more subtle and deep-rooted : our language, our ways of behaving, our institutions, all contribute in their respective ways to typify our culture, and it is important to recognize how we acquire them, the rôle they play and how they help us in a variety of ways to feel at ease amongst those of similar culture.

No-one is born with a built-in culture or way of life but only with the capacity to learn it. There is nothing peculiar about a European baby that dictates that it should find European languages easier than, say, African languages, that it should instinctively eat with knife and fork, prefer a balanced to a bulk diet or use a lavatory rather than an odd corner of the home out of sight. All these are aspects of European culture in one form or another and most differ from cultures found in Africa. Most have to be learned the hard way by European children growing up in a European culture and there is no evidence that an African or an Esquimo or an Indian child would learn them any more or less easily. While making the point that any child normally endowed can pick up the essentials of any known culture, one must not imply that the culture the child learns does not owe a great deal to the group of ancestors from which that child sprang. Culture grows and develops through the generations and is built up over time, often a very long time and largely by processes of which the individual is unaware.

It is by means of culture that the young learn to adapt themselves to their physical environment and to the people with whom they associate. Once learnt, culture becomes a way of life, the sure, familiar and largely automatic way of getting what the individual needs from the society in which he lives. This is achieved by providing a set of behaviour patterns that individuals brought up together recognise as the right and proper way of behaving. These behaviour patterns may be words, gestures, facial expressions, the knowledge of when to shake hands and when not to do so, all the various forms of greeting and the accepted responses to those forms, the methods of giving and receiving orders and knowing which remarks are to be taken seriously and which are not. These and a host of others are essential elements of our culture and they are as important to our composure as our religion or method of earning a living. They ensure that we feel at ease within our own community. They fulfill the functions of passwords or passports and once learned they become automatic. We take them completely for granted, so much so that it is improbable that we could analyse them in terms of our own culture ourselves. They give us a sense of security and status and they are reinforced by a variety of sanctions that ensure that we do not ignore or repudiate them. Those who do not abide by them are unacceptable and cease to belong.

It is cultural patterns of behaviour that largely determine the circle of people we accept as friends. Those people who have a common background, communicate in the way that we communicate and speak as we do are the more readily acceptable. They are the 'in' group of the psychologists; people in other professions or in other walks of life are less acceptable to us because they behave differently in given situations. In short, people are unacceptable primarily if they do not practice or accept one's own conventions. We then either refer to them as eccentric or as downright outsiders depending upon the extent of the variance of their behaviour.

This being the case it is perhaps natural that people should believe that their own culture represents the best and indeed the only sensible way of doing things. This is normal to most communities and psychologists refer to it as 'ethnocentricism', the belief that not only the culture but the nation or race to which the people belong forms the centre of the world. A more commonplace term for the same phenomena is parochialism. Individuals identify themselves with their own group and its ways to the extent that any criticism of them is taken as an affront not only to the individual but to the group. 'If you criticize my country, you are criticizing me. If you criticize me you are criticizing my country.' And with this attitude goes the tendency to attribute all individual peculiarities as national characteristics. By this process of stereotyping for example, do the Scots acquire their reputation for being mean, the Jews for being miserly, the Germans for being gluttons or French women for being provocative. If an Englishman does something odd or even anti-social in a foreign country, he is seen to behave thus because he is one of the eccentric English not because he is John Smith. He may be censured as an individual but his country is, at least in the public mind, censured as well. This stereotyping is a permanent characteristic of all national groups. We suffer as a result of it in other lands. We inflict our own version of it on other nationals.

All this is very relevant when people leave their own lands and settle down in a foreign country. They are subjected immediately to a series of shocks. All the familiar landmarks of social behaviour, the so well-known cues, are missing. The people of the host country, on the other hand, appear to lack the normal conventions of social behaviour. All the gestures, the expected forms of communication and the accepted ways of doing things are reversed or even unknown and they are replaced by a quite different and apparently illogical system. The newcomer feels like a fish out of water. Even if he hears what the local people say, he does not always understand what they mean. Nor is it only the different social conventions, the unusual behaviour of his hosts that is hard to understand and with which it may be very difficult to sympathize. There are very often real physical difficulties never before encountered. There is perhaps considerable discomfort resulting directly from the climate; there are new and often alarming maladies; there are dangers of special kinds not met with at home such as snakes and biting insects. There are servant troubles, accommodation troubles, transport troubles, together with a shortage of those ingredients, goods or services to which the visitor is accustomed. These troubles are more easily recognized and identified than are those connected with behaviour patterns or culture and are therefore the ones about which there is the most grousing. Thus, when foreigners get together in a strange land to grouse about the people of that country and their way of life, they are suffering from a malady to which the term culture shock has been given. There is, of course, considerable variation in individual degrees of culture shock. Some people, though very few, feel at home in a new environment from their very first day and they never change. At the other extreme are people who find it quite impossible to live away from the land of their birth even for a short time. Usually, however, people are too taken up by the novelty, the glamour, the excitement of a new place for them to think introspectively about themselves for some weeks or even months after they arrive. There is a kind of honeymoon period during which time they stay in hotels, meet only the local residents who speak their own language and who have, for various reasons, cause to please them. Important visitors probably never get beyond the honeymoon stage. They are pampered and petted wherever they go, they see only the best places and never meet the local trouble shooters if their hosts know their business. At the end of the tour they speak glowingly, at press conferences, of progress, goodwill and responsibility well-shouldered. Central Africa has seen such people, politicians in the majority, come and go for years.

But the sightseeing honeymoon period does not long survive if the foreign visitor remains and has to start coping with the day-to-day problem of normal, as distinct from tourist, life in his new home. Hostility to the local people is the first symptom that an individual is suffering from culture shock. The fact that the natives do not suffer from most of the hardships that beset the foreigner is readily translated into a feeling of dislike for them. They are seen as callous, indifferent, insensitive even if they are not actually blamed for many of the very real hardships that exist. The ways of the host country are seen as bad because they make the visitor feel bad and he very soon develops a hostile and aggressive attitude towards the indigenous people.

The next stage of culture shock through which the visitor passes can be called regression. The home environment, the familiar ways of living, the old and trusted ways of thinking, all suddenly assume tremendous importance. All the local difficulties and problems can be happily sunk in an orgy of nostalgic memories, shared for preference with others of like mind. This tendency to hold on to the ways and practices of the home country is found in many parts of the world. Social behaviour, language, beliefs are frozen at the level they had attained at the time the immigrants left their own country. Thus certain words still used today on the western seaboard of America, particularly in New England, were common in Shakespearean times but have long vanished from contemporary British usage. And many of the songs and legends of the negroes of the Southern States of America are today remembered only by the very oldest Africans living in the areas from which the slaves were carried. The survival of French culture in Mauritius or Quebec many decades after all formal links with France have been cut are further examples.

Stereotyping quietly follows from regression. This is something to which most people are prone in a mild way. But the visitor living abroad who reveals both regression and stereotyping has little hope of recovery. Once he sees his host in the form of a character, once he has developed in his mind's eye the typical French, the typical Russian, Turk, Italian or African, he never really finds his way back to normal social life with those whom he has so completely failed to understand.

The immigrant suffering from culture shock reveals other and more interesting personal symptoms. There is excessive washing of the hands, much concern over drinking water, food, dishes and bedding, fear of physical contact with attendants or servants, an absent-minded, far-away stare that is sometimes called the tropical stare, a feeling of helplessness and the desire for dependance upon long-term residents of the immigrant's own race or nationality; fits of anger over delays or other minor frustrations, an outright refusal to learn the language of the host country, an excessive fear of being cheated, robbed or injured, great concern over minor pains and eruptions of the skin.

Central Africa provides ample evidence of culture shock and the devastating consequences to all concerned of our failure to understand the true nature and reason for the behaviour of our fellow Europeans in this strife-strewn area. Here the physical difficulties are real enough. The climate is hot and dry for most of the year and extremely trying even for those who have lived many years in the area. The brochures that set out the features of the country, either to attract tourists or immigrants, never mention that in order to escape from this somewhat unpleasant climate most Europeans rise very early in the morning, often before five o'clock, and they are in bed and asleep by ten at night. To people not used to this kind of day it can be extremely difficult to adjust to such hours. Then there is the ever-present danger of bilhartzia for those who bathe in lakes or rivers, upsets of the stomach are frequent and the altitude is bad for hearts.

But it is in the social field that adjustment becomes most difficult. Even if there were no Africans at all in Central Africa there would be problems enough. This is because there are two types of European living side by side in the territories who come from two very different backgrounds. On the one hand are the pioneer settlers or their descendants and on the other hand there are the immigrants, the majority of whom have entered the area since 1946.

These two groups of people could hardly be more different. They are in their respective ways the products of different centuries. The pioneer is still a Victorian in outlook. He has a high moral code, he is not hurried and he does not easily change his way of life or his ambitions. He values money but most of those who survive have sufficient for them not to worry unduly about it. They do not particularly want it for its own sake or believe that status is gained by its possession. They are extremely conservative in the non-political sense and generally very satisfied with their niche in the world. In Southern Rhodesia, where most of them live, their world is bounded, apart from the needs of occasional holidays in Europe, by the Limpopo in the south and the Zambesi to the north.

Much has changed in Britain since the days, sixty or more years ago, when the pioneers set out for Rhodesia and the recent post-war immigrants tend to reflect those changes that have been for the worse rather than for the better. Many were more concerned with leaving England than in helping to build up a new continent. Few were possessed of any missionary ardour or sense of vocation. To some extent this tendency reflected the post-war needs of the territories. The explorer-come-adventurer was no longer needed. His rôle was completed. The need now was for capital, for artisans and for people in trade to help build up the new secondary industries that were to add a balance to an economy still too dependent upon farming and mining. It has been said that Central Africa received the N.C.O. and Kenya the Officer class after the war, a generalization that would not appear to be too wide of the mark. But perhaps the greatest tragedy was that many of those with capital, many of the craftsmen and many of the commercial people who migrated were themselves second-raters. Too many of the wealthy people who migrated were seeking only a comfortable life with the minimum of responsibility. Lower taxation and plenty of servants figured high in their objectives. Such people were of little use in England and became parasites in Rhodesia. Good craftsmen, for their part, did not have to leave England after the war to better their standard of living. The home country desperately needed such men and rewarded them well.

There would be every reason for pioneer settler and recent immigrant to antagonize each other considerably. A similar situation has of course happened in many parts of the world and is still happening every day. In the new towns of Britain, for example, the established residents with their often more leisurely pace resent the arrival of the new residents with their accent on change and progress. But in Central Africa hostility never became serious because of the close proximity to an overwhelming majority of Africans continually at their doorstep forced these two distinct types of European to close their ranks. The problems they have had to face in adjusting to each other are real enough, but they tend to be minimized by the difficulty both types of European experience in adjusting to the local Africans.

For African social behaviour, African culture, African manners, etiquette and conventions are based upon entirely different premises to those of western society. As a people the Africans set much store by politeness, by good manners and by courtesy. It often happens, however, that some of their behaviour is the direct opposite to what Europeans practice and believe to be right in similar situations. Thus to stand up in the presence of a superior is to the African an extremely impolite form of behaviour. He squats down to show his respect where we stand up. He holds out both his hands to express gratitude in a manner that to the European is extremely like asking for more. Then, much misunderstanding can arise where Europeans deal with members of tribes who have no word for 'thank you'. The Africans concerned are no less grateful for whatever they may have been given but they just have other ways, perfectly well understood amongst themselves, for showing their gratitude. Again, to Africans it is considered rude both to hurry or to knock on doors before entering. The former suggests that the person concerned has forgotten to start upon whatever errand he is engaged upon until too late, thus reflecting discourtesy to the person he is visiting. To knock upon a door suggests to the African, but not of course to the European into whose room he enters, that the person concerned is unaware of his presence. And this would imply a certain lack of perception. All this was quite suitable in tribal society where people could usually see a visitor coming from a long way off and where, in any case, there were no doors upon which to knock. These are forms of social behaviour that cannot bridge the gap and will have to change. But in the going they cause much friction to both sides, for there is so little mutual understanding.

The European preoccupation with time and the clock seems quite strange and indeed a little uncouth to Africans, who rate social graces far higher in their scale of values than adhering to a strict timetable. For example, when two Nyakuyusa elders meet in the road and say good morning to each other, it will involve a good twenty minutes exchange of formal phrases. Such behaviour derives from the fact that these Africans rate personal dignity very highly. They take the view that a man's deportment should be always grave and dignified. But when a European sends a member of the Nyakuyusa tribe on an errand, and the African does not return promptly because he happens perhaps to have met a friend on the road, the delay is easily put down either to idleness or disobedience.

There are also occasions at work when African values can cause both frustration and confusion. Brought up to put the needs of the members of their family before their own at all times, Africans will share what they have or what they earn with any near relative who happens to be at hand or in need. If two brothers are earning respectively ten pounds a week and two pounds a week, the brother earning the larger amount will think nothing of putting his full wages into a common pool until both have been able to buy, for example, a bicycle. By African logic each brother is contributing his full time to the acquisition of what he and his brother both need. Differential rewards for different degrees of skill was unknown in tribal society and so the European's habit of paying higher rates for one job than another is not considered good enough reason to flaunt their socially-approved convention. Such behaviour, of course, is quite beyond European understanding and in particular it makes a nonsense of incentive payments or offers of more cash for more work. It also makes marketing forecasts as to how many bicycles or other goods Africans in each income group can afford extremely unreliable.

Practices of this kind, and they are legion, are hard enough to live and work with even if there is a measure of sympathy on both sides. Such sympathy, however, does not exist and the whole situation is made worse because the political, economic and social structure of the territories all contrive in their respective ways to create the idea of the black man's inferiority. From his earliest youth the white man sees the black man as the servant, at the beck and call of anyone whose skin is white. African freedom of movement is restricted by law and all menial work is 'Kaffir' work, unfit for the individual who is fortunate enough to have been born with a white skin. In the same way and by a similar process of association, a bad stroke in a game of tennis is a 'kaffir' stroke, while a decent person who plays the game is a white man—even if his skin is jet black.

Obviously one cannot ascribe the whole of the Europeans' attitude towards Africans as due to culture shock. Much of it derives from ignorance or rationalisation. The African's gaiety, his quick smile and his inexperience of western ways all tend to lead Europeans into regarding him as a child in mental development. It suits the white settler very well to think this and the belief is reinforced in a variety of subtle ways. For example, lacking the necessary skills for living in the western form of society, it is easy enough for Europeans to imagine that the African is incapable of acquiring such skills. It is probably true to say that the vast majority of Europeans are quite genuine in believing that the African will never be their equal. And from this springs the idea that he has a basically low intelligence and that he lacks a sense of responsibility. Moreover his wholesale imitation of the white man is seen as yet further evidence of white superiority. And as imitations often produce incongruities the white man not only comes to despise but also to ridicule. The poorly-written letter, the misadventures of houseboys or cooks using unknown ingredients are all excellent material for dining out stories and help to build up the stereotype African in the European mind.

Ultimately, as Professor MacCrone points out, the white man sees the black 'not as an individual personality like himself, but as a representative of an alien group whose most striking characteristics are an inferiority in intelligence and knowledge, an inferiority in standards of living and occupation, a tendency towards violent and criminal practices, a behaviour which is childish and often ridiculous, in short, the opposite of all those qualities which form the image that the white man has in mind when he thinks of his own group. In spite of the numerous exceptions in both races, it is these images or concrete ideas, strongly charged with emotion, which determine the attitude of the white man both to members of his own group as well as to members of the alien group.'[1]

Behaviour of this kind reveals many of the symptoms of culture shock. And the aggressive attitude that follows the shock is also typical. Instead of trying to account for conditions as they really are by an honest analysis of the situation and the historical circumstances that have created it, the Europeans soon come to imagine that the problems of Africa have been created for their own especial annoyance. 'One could not understand Africans if one lived here a hundred years' is a remark often heard from settlers, but, also, and here is real tragedy, from Native Commissioners and others concerned with the direction of African affairs as well. The inference of this remark is further evidence of the inherent European belief that the African does not think rationally, that he is not predictable, that he is not really a human being in the sense that white men are.

Of course there is no short cut to understanding the profoundly different African way of life and the many difficulties that the African must overcome before the transition to a European way of living is achieved. For example, to get Africans who do not normally use the words 'thank you' in their own vernacular to express gratitude in the European manner, would either entail inventing a word for 'thank you' in their own language and then teaching them how that word would have to be used in the many social situations in which it occurs,

[1] 'Psychological Factors affecting the Attitude of White and Black in South Africa.' I. D. MacCrone, *S.A. Journal of Science*, Vol. XXVII, 1930.

or else teaching them not only to speak English but to think English also.

All this is far too laborious and Europeans resort to neither expedient. After hostility and stereotyping have developed, they withdraw within their own community and quickly equate their own way of doing things with their own superior material culture. From this springs the parochialism that almost every observer, irrespective of his political leanings, notes and comments upon. Few of the white inhabitants keep very much abreast of world problems or show any great interest if the conversation goes that way. They are completely absorbed in their somewhat narrow lives.

Regression can be seen in the way the original pioneers and their descendants still live. Their attitude to life, their philosophy and their morals are still heavily tinged with Victorianism. The design of their homes and their manner of furnishing them are all of an earlier age and because of this tendency to regression they see no cause to change.

Collectively both pioneer and recent immigrant speak of home and England in romantic terms that few Englishmen outside of Central Africa would recognise as contemporary England. It is said to be a place where the dignity of labour is still understood, where a man's word is his bond, where people give an honest day's work for an honest day's pay, where craftsmen abound.

Regression for women immigrants takes a different form to that found in their menfolk. For women, there are few of the ideals associated with craftsmanship or the dignity of labour. The husband, after all, goes to work in much the same way that he did in England and the work environment, apart from the heat, is itself not dissimilar. But the wife has to operate for most of the day in an environment very different to anything she has known before. She is usually in much closer daily contact with Africans than is her husband. The shock for her is consequently correspondingly greater and for her, regression takes the form of a longing for queues, for rationing, for phone calls to mother and for doing all her own housework. It is the wives who are mostly the cause of families returning to England after a few years in Rhodesia. The remedy, of course, lies in letting the wife go home on her own just once. That is all she needs, for back home she soon tires of the familiar round and quickly finds much merit in living in a home where all the housework is done by servants, where almost every material advantage is available and where, when one feels tired, one can lie down and stay there until one feels better.

The final stage of culture shock, the tendency to see the local people in stereotype form, is very pronounced. Few Europeans come in contact with Africans other than their cook, gardener or office messenger. On the behaviour of these limited few, therefore, they base their judgement of the contemporary African. Nor do they see many of his better qualities or understand the difficulties he faces in adjusting to their so different way of life. They pick upon his mistakes, his drinking or his womanizing to brand all Africans with the same label. Sixpence the cook may be quite a man amongst his fellows and in his own environment, but his odd name and the various mistakes he makes with unfamiliar kitchen ingredients soon becomes the basis for many a good story of African stupidity.

Central Africa none the less is very much on the move. The physical face of the towns and small communities change almost overnight, as new capital is brought in for development and quickly-made fortunes are expended on status-giving possessions. Even the nonentity is carried forward in the surge. The pace is breathless and the confusion of life in so rapidly changing, supposedly classless society, in which so little is sure save that the salary cheque will continue for the present to be larger than most people ever dreamt of—all this is difficult enough to adjust to with composure. Add the over-riding menace of the African who has long reacted to hostility with hostility and the dilemma of the settler is clear enough. He is out of his depth, all the familiar props have been knocked away. His reaction is the same as countless other communities have revealed in roughly similar conditions. And his parochialism, his almost hysterical cry to be left alone to work out his own destiny are both in their respective ways advanced symptoms of culture shock.

Perhaps the white man's greatest tragedy is that he is misunderstood in those quarters from which he should expect the greatest help. He is blamed for his attitude to the African and for the racial policy that he follows. In fact, of course, this racial policy is only a symptom of an underlying malaise and the cause has to be sought much deeper. The settler community would react very much as they do now whether the native peoples of Central Africa were brown, yellow, or even colourless.

CHAPTER 4

The African at Home

Culture shock is one of the reasons for Europeans in Central Africa behaving as they do. The Africans themselves also exert a considerable influence. Were the Europeans to attempt to understand the Africans around them, the situation would be a lot easier than it is. But although the facts are available for those who care to study them, the Europeans as a group continue to hold that African behaviour is illogical and beyond understanding. 'I have lived here all my life, old boy, and believe me you'll never get to the bottom of a native's mind.' How often does the newcomer meet this and similar phrases, phrases that are none the less wrong for all that they are sometimes not unkindly expressed.

Yet it is essential for the interested observer to understand the African if he is to understand the European. Nor is this understanding of the African so very difficult, for his behaviour is quite logical within the framework of his own environment. It is logical but also quite different to much that is found in European society. And as his behaviour is different so the African himself is different also. It may be unfashionable to assert that Africans are different in a world that pledges itself to work for the elimination of all racial differences and discriminations and the social theories that grow from such beliefs. Africans none the less are different from Europeans and it has to be said and understood, if policy decisions are to be based upon facts and not upon sentiment. The differences are of the kind that make the Briton different from the Frenchman and more different still from the Russian. They are not differences due to any biological factors but solely due to environment. They can be eliminated once both groups find themselves living under similar circumstances with equal privileges and equal responsibilities. But they cannot be quickly eliminated by offering the African the material trappings of western civilization on a plate.

The problems that arise from Africans and Europeans behaving and thinking differently are further complicated by the fact that the Africans themselves are of two very distinct kinds. There are those who live in tribal communities in the native reserves and whose ways of living have not been radically altered by contact with Europeans. Secondly there are those who have left their homes and become in varying degrees detribalized. Both types are important for different reasons and both must be understood. The first commands attention because tribal thinking still influences the thinking and behaviour of

The African at Home

the detribalized. And the detribalized Africans are important because it is they, few though they may be relatively, who matter politically. It is they who make what Europeans refer to as 'all the trouble'.

Any short account of tribal society in Central Africa must of necessity generalize. Tribes differ profoundly amongst themselves. Some are organized into large kingdoms with all the trappings of government. Others operate in smaller but mutually dependant units. Some range over wide areas herding cattle while others practise agriculture in a relatively small compass. Religious beliefs differ and marriage and social customs vary enormously. In some tribes descent is reckoned through the mother, in others it is through the father. Some are warlike and others have always been lovers of peace. But however they live, all tribes share one common problem and their reaction to this problem is very much the same in every case. Africa is a country of immensely heavy rains, of long periods of drought, of food shortages, pestilences and many diseases. The elements are hard and all African tribes react in much the same manner to them because they understand very little of the forces of nature against which they must constantly exercise their puny strength.

In societies that have no knowledge of scientific principles it is necessary for certain ways of living to be tested by trial and error and then followed without change or interruption lest an unsuccessful experiment should lead to complete disaster. For example, having found that crops planted in November can usually be relied upon to prosper, November planting becomes the inflexible rule. To plant a few months later or to change the hunting ground on the whim of some innovator, is far too dangerous a practice to encourage.

Conservatism therefore conditions every aspect of tribal life. It is extolled in tales and stories, it is an integral part of tribal education. There were no rules specifically demanding conformity, no commandments that said 'thou shalt not change', but there were very binding forces at work to ensure that men did not become restless or seek to find better ways of doing things. Tribal religion was perhaps the principal agent. Public opinion and a variety of material rewards also played their part.

Here then lay the fundamental difference from the European way of life. Western civilization with its emphasis on a monetary acquisitive economy is essentially a risk-taking culture. But it is able to weigh the chances of a risk in the light of scientific information, so that success occurs at least as often as failure. European man, then, is bred in a risk-taking, highly individualistic community, in which status is achieved by getting ahead of one's fellows. The African finds his status by remaining in his rut. In so doing he sacrificed the possible advantage of progress and increasing wealth for the certainty of survival and by so doing he was able to effect as near perfect a system of social security—admittedly at a somewhat low level by world standards—as is found in any land.

There were no atheists or free-thinkers in tribal society and no one questioned the tribal religion. Every tribe had its god or gods and its own form of heaven. For some heaven was vaguely somewhere in the sky, for others it was more precisely beneath a certain piece of land. In this later case the burial place of the ancestors acquired considerable importance and became hallowed ground. The chief was usually the focal point of tribal religion. Usually he combined the rôle of secular and sacred leader of his people. Where this was the case, succession to the chieftainship was closely prescribed and either followed in a family or as a result of divine indication. The chiefs or priests, if there were any, were expected to provide guidance against all the dangers and perils to which the tribe might be subjected. By spells and prayer or by offerings they claimed that they could ensure rain, success in battle or freedom from disease. Where they succeeded they were respected for their skill; when they failed, they were not immediately discredited. It was felt that a being more powerful than they had opposed them, or the gods to whom they appealed had not wished their prayers answered. Such things were accepted as inevitable in a world inhabited by supernatural beings whose support could never be relied upon. Unless the chief or priest was frequently unsuccessful he was not therefore discredited.

In western civilization it has been the increase of scientific knowledge that has accounted largely for the disappearance of magical practices. We now have our children immunized when there is the threat of a diphtheria epidemic, whereas not so many hundred years ago our ancestors used to burn an old woman at the stake when faced with the same danger. These ancestors of ours were not obsessed with the fear of witches, nor did they live their lives under the shadow of witchcraft and magic. Africans are the same. They used magic or religious practices to a practical end. The tribal hunter might know just where to find his quarry, he might have great skill with spear or bow and arrow and be confident of his strength. But he could never be sure that a puff of wind might not deflect his aim, that a snake might not be laying in the path he took or that some beast might not give warning of his approach to the creature he was stalking. The hunter, therefore, muttered certain spells and performed certain observances before setting out. These magical practices increased his confidence but did not lead him to reduce his endeavours or relax his care.

Tribal religion had one other vital rôle. It sanctified the *status quo*. Good and bad could be termed the known and the unknown, the usual and the unusual, the expected and the unexpected. People who did the expected things, the approved things, the usual things could

The African at Home

expect supernatural aid. Those who attempted the unknown ran the double risk of failure and divine wrath. Typical of how religion sanctified the *status quo* is the Balayia prayer that asked their God to 'Let things take their normal course' and more specifically to 'let the sun shine as usual'.

As in western civilization, family life is the cornerstone of tribal organization. There is, of course, a considerable diversity of practice in such matters as descent and inheritance in how authority is delegated and whether a young married couple should live with the parents of the bride or the bridegroom. But these variations of practice are of local importance only. The significant features of African family life are that the family unit is very large and that a very strong measure of mutual help is expected from its members.

Rules of this kind are essential for survival. It would be impossible for an African family unit comprising father, mother and children to carry on for long in isolation. Were the father to have an accident or die, the remaining members of the family would soon perish. To depend upon a single individual is too grave a risk and so in almost all tribal communities the family unit is very much more than the group we recognize in Europe as constituting a normal family. Although the home itself may contain only parents and children, a large number of relatives are never far away and are always on call to any member who requires help. Moreover in an environment in which a small family cannot expect to survive, a single person would have no hope at all. There were no single unattached people, therefore, in African communities. Single men remain with their parents until they marry after which they either continue to live with their parents or they go and live with their wife's parents. As soon as a girl reaches puberty she is expected to marry and she passes from the care of one family group to that of another. Widows are the responsibility of one of their late husbands' surviving brothers or male relatives and old people are assiduously cared for by their children.

The need for corporate community effort is constant and in order to ensure that individuals recognized their obligations to each other an elaborate system of what are called 'classificatory relationships' has been built up. Children call all their father's brothers by the single term of 'father'. In the same way their father's sisters and mother's sisters are called 'mother'. All male cousins are called brother and all female cousins sister. This general use of terms normally denoting only close relatives does not in any way reduce the strong bonds that exist between children and their real fathers and real mothers, brothers and sisters. It just serves to ensure in a most telling manner that every member of the tribe recognize obligations and know where to go for help.

The position of women in African tribal society has been particularly badly misinterpreted. At one extreme is the view that women occupy, or once did occupy, a dominant position associated with the term matriarch. Nobody would seriously defend this idea today, but many people still believe the opposite extreme, that women in tribal society occupy a degraded position in that they are bought and sold like chattels at the whim of greedy parents or avaricious suitors and that to their lot falls all the dull and heavy work. Here it is necessary to distinguish between theory and practice. It is quite true that in terms of the legal rules operating in most primitive communities, women occupy a subordinate position, but this has to be offset by other considerations, considerations of what actually happens. There must, of course, be differences in the rôles played by men and women in any society. For obvious reasons, women must invariably be concerned with the home and young children and men with obtaining food and providing protection. Very broadly, there is a tendency to allocate dangerous tasks and those requiring strenuous and concentrated physical effort for comparatively short periods of time to men. Women are usually found undertaking the more prolonged but less concentrated type of work. This type of work fits admirably into their overall family responsibilities.

Some divisions of labour between the sexes can often be explained in terms of the above. Other practices are not so logical. In some tribes the making of pottery is men's work, in others it is undertaken by the women. Women of one tribe do the ploughing and in another it is the preserve of the men. Cows are sometimes milked by men and sometimes by women. These various differences are unimportant in a general way or for the better understanding of women's place in African society. The only time that they really give trouble is when a woman belonging to a tribe in which, say, ploughing is the men's preserve, marries into a community where the women are expected to plough. In circumstances of this kind she is greatly distressed. For one thing she has not the necessary training and for another, she does not know all the various magico-religious practices associated with ploughing in her husband's tribe that are held to be necessary for almost every type of work.

Beliefs about the African women's lower status are based to a large extent upon misinterpretation of certain marriage customs, and in particular on the idea of arranged marriages, the bride-price and polygamy. But these customs have to be seen against the background of African and not European marriage, against the background of African society and not European society.

The system of 'lobolo' or bride-price as it has been translated incorrectly, has been much criticized as being the purchase of a wife and, therefore, a degrading institution. In fact it is nothing of the kind. Its purpose is solely to readjust the balance when one family gains a daughter. When she goes to her new home she is immediately an economic asset. Her child-bearing capacity and her capacity for work will enrich the members of her husband's family. This upsets the equilibrium between the two families immediately. So there is a transfer of wealth when the daughter passes to her husband's family to ensure that the equilibrium is maintained. In earlier days the girl's family were given cattle and usually the number of beasts was strictly defined. These cattle would be regarded as belonging to their new owners only in trust. Should the girl prove barren, the cattle would have to be returned. If she only bore one child, then a proportion of the cattle would be sent back and after five children most tribes regarded the lobolo cattle as being honoured. These lobolo cattle were usually the property of the dead ancestors and could only be exchanged for a wife for one of the younger sons. The cattle also served as an instrument for stabilizing the marriage, since neither party wished to incur the anger of their respective ancestors by cancelling the arrangement and having to return the cattle. Both were, therefore, interested in ensuring that the marriage prospered. If the wife felt that she was being badly treated she could return home to her family and the chief might well rule that the lobolo cattle need not be returned, as the family had suffered a slight. Lobolo therefore helped to maintain the prestige and well-being of the wife once she had left her own home.

Perhaps the main difference between African and European marriage is that the idea of romantic love does not occur amongst the Africans. Marriage for them is a serious economic arrangement, conducted between two families for their mutual benefit. For this reason parents frequently decide together who their respective children shall marry, often before the children reach marriageable age. Frequently they will bring pressure to bear to impose such marriages when one or other of the two parties may be reluctant to entertain the idea. Such pressure is, however, rare as in a community in which most people think alike, family obligations are recognized by young people as matters of course. In most cases the individuals would no more think of opposing a marriage partner chosen for them than Europeans would think of protesting because they did not have a choice of parents. It is true that an arranged marriage is a restriction on liberty, but it is not the sort of liberty Africans have ever thought of demanding. And in any case, it bears as heavily on the man as on the woman. In a society in which cultural standards are common to all age groups and where there is no such thing as a 'new idea' or 'modern thinking' and no 'angry young men', the advantages of a particular choice made by elderly relatives are likely to be acknowledged by the young people concerned.

The young man seeks a bride who will be industrious, tidy and who looks capable of bearing many children. These are the qualities that he values and they are also the qualities his family value. That he does not seek affection, love, common interests or whatever Europeans may seek in their mates does not necessarily mean that there is a lack of common affection in African marriages. But as a rule this affection is a later growth. The couple fall in love after they have been married and not before. This is recognized as right and proper and is well illustrated in a story told by an anthropologist working amongst the Bemba. To the question of whether a man who had just married was fond of his wife, the reply was given, 'How can he be fond of her? How can he know what her heart is like until they have grown old together?'

Indeed there is ample evidence that husbands and wives in tribal Africa had very great affection for each other. But this never showed on the surface, as it does in European society. Decorum and etiquette decree that gestures of love and affection should never be made publicly. Husbands and wives are, for example, never seen even to hold hands in public. To their thinking, the European husband who kisses his wife goodbye on the steps of his house before leaving for work could not be more indecent if he were to make love to her as publicly.

Polygamy is relatively rare in Africa today for a variety of reasons that in the main relate to the break-up of tribal life. But, until the intrusion of a monetary economy and the availability of work for women in European employment, the majority of adult men were polygamously married. This practice has also been cited as typical of the inferior position occupied by African women. It must however be seen against the broad background of tribal society and the many problems that it faced. To think of it primarily in terms of sexual union is to misunderstand it completely. First was the question of surplus women normal in any society. To that must be added the fact that as the men performed most of the dangerous work, mortality was somewhat higher in their case than in the case of women. African society provided for these surplus women by arranging for their marriage to an appropriate man. In the event of a man dying it was usual for a surviving brother or male relative to take over the wives and it was expected that women transferred in this way would be accorded all the privileges they had previously enjoyed with their first husband. That is to say, the man could not ill-treat them or oblige them to perform tasks not normally prescribed for women. He might or he might not have intercourse with them, but if he should choose to do so the position was not as unhappy for the women concerned as it might be in western society, where a romantic attachment is regarded as a pre-requisite to sexual enjoyment.

From all accounts polygamous families ran fairly smoothly. This was for a variety of reasons peculiar to African society. In the first place the wives were very often sisters and had much in common. Then, too, each kept their own small homestead a distinct social unit with children and cooking arrangements her own preserve. The rights of each woman were also socially recognized and respected by her husband for fear of alienating public opinion or incurring the wrath of the tribal deities. That African women felt no sense of inferiority is shown by the fact that a wife would often beg her husband to take a second wife in order to lighten her domestic and economic tasks.

In his attitude to work and to the rewards for work done, Africans differed from Europeans in two important respects. First, they did not use money as a means of barter for goods or services. They paid either in kind or, more usually, in services. Secondly, there was strong social disapproval of any man who tried to better himself or his family above the accepted and prescribed level.

The absence of money does not call for comment, but the refusal to tolerate the ambitious man is fundamental in tribal philosophy and is above all else the cause for their being different.

To have allowed an economic free-for-all would have undoubtedly raised the standards of living of many tribesmen, but it would have left some, and perhaps many, behind in the race, and tribal society did not like individual loose ends in its social organization. Above all such a free-for-all could, in a community that had little or no knowledge of the laws of cause and effect, and in which a constant battle must be waged against the forces of nature, prove disastrous. Rightly perhaps in the circumstances, tribal society chose to play safe and not give the more able members the opportunity to better themselves above the level of their fellows. The penalty of such a choice was, of course, stagnation, but none questioned the choice. A way of living had been devised that gave a generally acceptable standard of living. It was felt to be good because nobody knew any better and society was so organized that nobody ever had the chance of knowing any better. African aspirations were never raised above their capacity to produce. In a variety of ways and from their earliest days, young people were taught to appreciate their lot and to fear changing it for something potentially better. How different is the training of young Europeans. To them the prize goes to the swiftest and only comparatively recently has public opinion seriously concerned itself collectively with the hindmost.

It is not only ambition that drives a European to work harder and to desire to take the first prize. There are also a number of other complex and interlocking factors. Chief of these are the desire for status, that is achieved by the possession of wealth, and the achievement of security in the future.

The motives prompting an African to work were quite different, although just as natural to his way of living as are the motives of Europeans to theirs. The African never thought of the future in terms of saving up or putting by. Had he done so individually he would inevitably have caused a dislocation in tribal equilibrium, for there would have been some individuals more successful than others, and some again who were not successful at all. There were, therefore, four good reasons why he made no provision for the time ahead. The first was this question of equilibrium. Secondly, there were no facilities for storing up possessions above a certain minimum subsistence level. Thirdly, any surplus that could be built up would always be something of an invitation to plunder by a tribe or group more powerful than the saver's own. Finally, very few people grew to an old age in which they became enfeebled or incapacitated, and the few who did live beyond sixty years were so few that they were rarely a burden upon the community. Quite the reverse, in fact, for these few were rated highly for their council and more than earned whatever it cost in terms of other men's labours to keep them.

The desire for status that is so powerful a driving force in western society also worked very differently in African tribal society. The African sought status but he found it more directly in work well done rather than in the amount he might earn by doing it. There was never a rate for the job, but each man would give of his best or do the kind of work for which his training had fitted him. His reward was the respect of his fellows and the sure knowledge that if in one instance he may have contributed more than they, he in his turn would, on balance, come to benefit from whatever they might do in the near or more distant future for him. Need was the criterion in any rewards that might be distributed for work done. A married man with a large family could expect to take home a larger share of the produce jointly harvested than a single man or one with only few dependants.

Work itself was so very different. It was periodic and largely seasonal in character. For women, perhaps, it was much as it is for the women of any race, since the caring for children and the preparation of meals must be a constant pre-occupation. But there was no regular daily routine for men with a timetable of work dictated by the clock. It mattered little whether a hunting party set off at nine or ten in the morning, and agricultural work, since it sought only to produce a sufficiency and not a surplus, would rarely occupy a full day. It could therefore be started late in the morning if the need arose. Hard and onerous work was shared and when completed there was usually a party at which the contributions of each individual might be toasted successively by the others, until all fell into a well-earned if sometimes alcoholic sleep.

Whereas European man is economic man, African man was social man. Europeans have their carrots and their sticks to prompt harder work and both are in large measure economic in operation. Africans too had their carrots and their sticks, but the incentives to which they responded and the sanctions that drove them were almost all of a social nature. Men worked for their fellows, knowing that so long as they played the tribal game the tribe would always care for them and that they would never suffer privations in greater measure than any of their fellows. And as people work better for their own kith and kin, rather than for strangers, tribal society ensured that there should always be a wide range of people whose relationship to each other was, as far as nomenclature could achieve, of a very close nature.

There was no special love of work in African society any more than there is anywhere else in the world, but Africans worked hard when it was necessary to work and when there was no work they enjoyed their leisure. Europeans have a somewhat puritanical approach to work. It is believed to be good in itself, or to be divinely ordained as part of man's lot. Proverbs and religion extol it in most Christian communities and if nothing else, it is seen as a means of keeping people out of mischief. Africans were probably less prone to get into what is currently called mischief during their periods of leisure, if only because there could be very little privacy in the kind of lives they led. That the devil might find a use for idle hands they conceded, but, on the whole, they found better ways than work to prevent him gaining too much of a hold. Work to them was, therefore, very specifically a means to an end and nothing more than that. It held no glory in itself.

Law and authority were vested in tradition and there were few offenders in a society that set so much store by conformity. In the absence of police, or law enforcement officers, this respect for the *status quo,* together with a very effective fear of supernatural anger should the laws be broken, contrived to keep the number of evildoers to a minimum. In civil cases as well as those that were of a more criminal nature, compensation of the injured party was considered more important than the punishment of the offender. A thief would be called upon to make good the loss he had caused, a murderer would in one form or another have to make a contribution to the family of his victim that would compensate for the loss of its member. In such cases the first need was to restore the equilibrium that existed between the accused and the injured party.

Chiefs and elders who administered the law were in many instances old men and such people were, in any case, likely to favour the traditional and the trusted method rather than the novel and the untried. The status accorded to age provided yet a further brake on young men who showed any inclination to use initiative. Not only were tribal councillors old men, but, in many cases, it was almost impossible for anyone but an old man to become chief. This was achieved by a form of succession that passed the chieftainship on to the oldest surviving male relative of the dead chief. Thus, when a chief died, first claim would go to any of his father's male relatives and should there be none of these alive then the chieftainship would pass to any surviving brothers. Only if there were no brothers left would the sons inherit. This principal established and maintained a permanent rule of old men.

It is possible to describe the typical African of tribal days fairly accurately. He was exactly the kind of person that the society in which he lived decreed that he should be. He was essentially conservative in how he thought and how he behaved; he valued very highly his family ties; he respected old age and both young and old set much store by individual good manners. He loved his children more, perhaps, than he ever came to love his wife. But on balance he was a good husband. He was deeply religious, quite unconcerned about his material future and he lacked any urge to better himself or engage in any kind of economic competition with those about him. He liked to be well thought of by his fellows but he never saw any merit in having more goods than he could usefully use. He had better ways of enhancing his status. In short, he was probably rather a nice person, if perhaps dull and unimaginative by western standards. He was certainly a very different kind of person to the stereotype African that has grown up in the minds of traders, employers of native labour, settlers of many kinds, even administrators and missionaries. To these Europeans, because they failed to understand the motives that prompted him, or the bonds that held him in check, he was seen as superstitious, irrational, lazy, immoral and of a childish or at least adolescent mentality.

Yet these same Europeans, probably the majority by far in Central Africa today, credit him with extraordinary psychological powers, such as a gift of telepathy, or the capacity to predict events—particularly the date of his own death. There is no evidence that the African possessed any of these latter qualities and he would be the last to claim them for himself. One assertion that is often made is that he is cruel, and perhaps by certain standards (lived up to by few nations in the world) he was. At the time Europeans first entered Rhodesia, the raids of the Matabele on local subordinate tribes were undoubtedly cruel and ruthless. Warriors gloried in slaughter for its own sake and it mattered little if the victims were women, children or old people provided they were of an enemy tribe. And, before infanticide came to be punished by the European authorities with the death penalty, it was customary for certain tribes to kill twins in a particularly horrible way. In these tribes, the mother of the children pushed earth down their throats with a small stick until they died, the idea being that as twins were unusual and thus abnormal they were dangerous and had to be killed.

Such behaviour horrifies us today and we feel it to be barbaric. But we sometimes forget that it is less than three hundred years since it was the practice in Europe to drive a stake through the heart of a person believed to be a vampire. And it is less than two hundred years since an Englishman in India mentioned quite casually in a report to London that it was the custom of his people to flog men to death for petty offences that carried the death penalty in England. Going back a little further, Cromwell's exploits are still to this day remembered with a shudder in Ireland and of course history records many other examples of barbaric cruelty in every European country. Indeed, the past twenty years in Germany and Russia have witnessed events as cruel as anything Africa could once rival.

It would seem that pity and what we call common humanity are in fact qualities of relatively recent growth. They flourish best where there is leisure and a certain degree of comfort. Where life is hard and callous, as for example in medieval Europe and tribal Africa, men harden their hearts to the suffering of others in rough proportion to the degree of discomfort to which they are accustomed. But, even today, when life in England is no longer brutal, there are odd inconsistencies of attitude. People are relatively unmoved by the atomic bombing and the slaughter of tens of thousands of Japanese, yet those same people band together and show every sign of real distress when they hear of old horses being shipped from Ireland to France in conditions of some discomfort to the horses concerned. Africans see Europeans as not only inconsistent in this respect but particularly cruel in a manner that they themselves find it difficult to understand. Thus when the B.B.C. announcer asks for the whereabouts of a man or woman who has not seen a dying mother or father for many years, we reveal to the African a callousness that is beyond their comprehension. To Africans a people who can allow their old parents to fend for themselves and die alone, can have no right to criticize anybody else for their cruelty.

All that the tribal African was, his good and his bad points, he owed to the type of society in which he lived. He can no more take credit for this system than can Britain take credit for its special system of parliamentary government. Centuries ago the idea of a parliament of commoners occurred to a small coterie of Englishmen. They could not possibly have conceived how their idea was to bear fruit and how, from such modest beginnings, the present House of Commons and the system of democratic parliamentary government that it houses would one day emerge and spread around the world.

In much the same way has tribal society evolved and grown until every custom, idea or belief has come to fulfill some interrelated function in which the rights and the obligations of each individual are carefully balanced. This balance is, however, a rigid one and herein lies the danger. The breakdown of one idea or institution is fatal to the whole, and western civilization, and in particular the concept of individual free enterprise with which it is so heavily percolated, has caused not one but many tribal institutions to disintegrate. The enforced removal of chiefs who happened also to be secular leaders of their people has divorced the tribe from their gods. Where the people have been moved away from land in which their ancestors lay buried there has been yet another blow at tribal religion. Cash wages have enabled individuals to contract out of their family obligations by either enabling them to be independent of the help of their fellows, or, possibly, to employ another to do their work for them. All this has seriously weakened family cohesion. The separation of a man and wife in European employment from their joint families has removed one of the most stabilizing agents in tribal marriage, and the elaborate division of labour between the sexes that was so carefully balanced to ensure full co-operation between the marriage partners breaks down completely when the men leave home for months on end to seek work on mines or in the European towns. Religious observances, particularly those associated with family life, can no longer be fully performed when the men are away from home and the women, left alone with responsibilities far beyond their training, often given up the hard struggle and move to town themselves.

The economic philosophy of the west coupled with the administrative measures imposed by colonial governments have successively and effectively destroyed tribal life. What survives has no longer balance or the capacity to survive on its own. It is kept going by every form of first aid a charitable government can provide. But it is now an artificial creation, without loyalties or traditions, waiting only for its final demise.

It is quite erroneous to blame the missions for this break-up of tribal organization. 'Before the missionaries got hold of him the African was a decent sort,' is a remark much repeated by European settlers. It is certainly true that in many instances the missionaries were the first white people to set foot in tribal lands, but the conversions they achieved were few and far between. Livingstone, for all the great work he achieved and the deep affection he gained from the Africans themselves, can hardly have won more than a dozen adherants to the Christian faith. In the early days there was much that the missionaries could do in the field of medicine and education, but there was little or no need for the faith that they also offered.

This the Africans possessed in abundance and theirs was a system of belief that was all embracing. It gave them complete assurance and security. The Christian faith might, as the missionaries suggested, give more comfort in the world hereafter, but it could not offer its converts anything particularly comfortable or assured during their lives because they immediately cut themselves adrift from their fellows upon whom they ultimately relied for their security.

Few of the Africans' good qualities, his sharing with relatives, his patience and his cheerfulness were likely to prosper or even survive in the strongly economic, competitive and highly materialistic world of the west that he has been compelled to enter. Ironically, that same western world is today striving to achieve what it regards as a better social order than it now possesses, one in which every man shall enjoy an adequate measure of social security, in which men will give of their skill without asking for differential rewards greater than their less gifted colleagues can expect. The African had all these things in tribal life; his system of social security was proof against any but the most devastating of natural disasters. The idea of differential rewards was unthinkable to him. Every man served his own community to the best of his ability and put his own interests after those of his fellows. Yet he must give up all this, become a slave to clock and wage packet, before he can find again the security in a new kind of society that is now attempting to achieve the same values that he once knew.

For the tribal African the transition to the western way of life is full of difficulties. He meets his own kind of culture shock and his reactions are in their way similar to that of the Europeans. He is eager to learn more of the European world and at the same time he fears contact with it. So he clings to many of his traditional beliefs and practices as a drowning man clings to a straw.

CHAPTER 5

Bad Citizens

If the tribal African is in many ways different from the European and therefore not easy to understand, the African who lives in town is even more so. Superficially, these urban Africans resemble Europeans in many ways. They live in the same kind of houses, they work an eight to nine-hour day five or six days a week, their clothes, their furnishings, many of their divertisements and their needs are similar, if all on a somewhat different scale. But this apparent similarity is deceptive. It does not go very deep, but deep enough for the white settlers to make all manner of assumptions about Africans that are quite invalid. European-type clothes, town planning, plumbing, regular hours of work and a balanced diet have in fact done surprisingly little to change tribal attitudes to life and the majority of urban Africans differ from the Europeans in whose midst they live for most of the reasons already referred to in the case of their tribal cousins. In addition, there are a variety of social, economic and political factors that render the African growing up in town as liable to his own particular form of culture shock as are the Europeans themselves. Misunderstandings occur, therefore, on both sides. The more sophisticated Africans do not understand why it is that Europeans living in the Federation do not behave towards them as do the white people in England. The unsophisticated African is not in a position to make such a comparison. He just does not like the attitude of his white masters. Europeans, for their part, consider the urban Africans bad citizens and unwilling workers. Both these two major criticisms of the urban African are largely true.

As ever in a descriptive account of this kind it is necessary to generalize. About the tribal African generalization is to some extent fair because tribal life established a fairly rigid pattern for all to follow. But generalizing about the detribalized urban African can be dangerous unless it is recognized from the start that there will be many Africans who do not fit into any recognized pattern at all. There are a few who have adjusted not only in their living but also in their thinking to the European pattern. There are those who have made no adjustments at all. There are Africans educated up to university dergee level and there is much illiteracy. There are rich Africans and many who are desperately poor. There are many good men, good by any standards, who have no riches and no education. There are others who are well read and well endowed but who are bad by any standards. In the same way there are towns in which Africans have been allowed to make much headway and others where every sort of restriction has been imposed. There are also good and bad European masters, good and bad laws, all of which influence the urban African in different ways. No attempt can be made therefore to categorize all this diversity. It is, however, possible to strike a balance and show how heavily are the scales loaded against the urban African in his attempt at adjustment and why, in consequence, the European feels and behaves as he does.

Nationalism and the pressure of world opinion are the African's obvious allies and in the long term they must be his salvation. But for the present they are still very distant and not too easy to turn to profitable account. Europeans bent upon defending the *status quo* make much of the advantages they have brought to the African. They quote the vast sums spent on his education, on his health and on his housing. And of course there are valid assets. But to the African the manner of their giving is suspect and considerable though the sums may be that are spent, they are still usually grossly inadequate. His overcrowded home, the queue at the outpatients' clinic, the paltry wage packet, coupled with the political and economic discrimination to which he is subjected at every turn, far outweigh any other considerations. He grumbles at what he does not have rather than rejoicing at what the charity of his European masters has made available to him. In this he is very much the same as other peoples in other lands who have lived in similar straits. Sadly enough the Europeans in Central Africa have ignored the history books in their search for a solution to the problem of handling a proletariat.

Far more than any material assets, the African needs sympathy and encouragement in his attempt to make the jump from tribal to the western way of life. To adapt himself to the western economic system while at the same time being hedged about by all manner of discriminatory obstructions specially placed there by European governments or their representatives, requires almost miraculous powers of adaptability. So the path is long and tortuous and to the casual observer it is not even very well attempted.

The difficulties that the African meets can be classified as economic, social and political. Housing, for example, is obviously one of the social aspects but like each of his other problems it is not wholly social. It has economic and political aspects as well. Housing is actually the African's most apparent pressing need although they themselves might not put it top of the list nor even recognize the warping effect that overcrowded conditions impose on their personalities. Many accept overcrowded homes as normal of the urban way of life. The country folk who migrated to the industrial areas of Britain in the eighteenth and nineteenth centuries no doubt felt the same. Yet when Winston Churchill wrote, many years ago, that

'We shape our houses and they in turn shape us', he was making a profound sociological observation as relevant in Africa today as in Britain at the time of which he was writing. African housing in many areas has to be seen to be believed. On the large copper mines it is probably at its best. It is at its worst around the larger municipalities where overcrowding is so much more in evidence.

Every European town, mining camp or farm has its African residential area. On the whole the Europeans do not particularly like to live too close to African settlements but the nature of their mutual obligations makes this necessary. Africans cannot be expected to travel long distances each morning and evening to work unless their transport is heavily subsidized. And municipalities or mining authorities are usually unwilling to shoulder this responsibility.

The larger African townships, or locations as they are sometimes termed, lying on the outskirts of Salisbury, Bulawayo or Lusaka, and around the large mines on the Copper Belt of Northern Rhodesia, give the impression of being fully developed towns in their own right. There are rows of shops, pleasant tree-lined avenues with detached bungalows along each side. Many of the gardens are well tended. Behind this façade are rows of smaller houses, often only single rooms, in which are accommodated the single men. Beer halls are favourite centres of recreation. There are cinemas, churches, even garages. The shops themselves reveal much of the variety of a European town. There are groceries, butchers, bakers, cycle repair shops, secondhand furniture shops, carpenters, tailors, builders. In the larger African towns there is every apparent prospect of community life developing. On the smaller mines or around the small European towns where there are few factories or commercial organizations and where only African domestic servants are required, there is not the same diversity and here a varied community life is of course not possible.

Each African township, however large it may be, and some accommodate over 100,000 people, is completely dependent upon the European economy. If the Europeans prosper, then the African town grows too. If the Europeans run into economic difficulties, then African prosperity falls proportionately. In no cases are the African townships capable of individual self development. Legislation makes this virtually impossible. Africans rarely own the land on which their homes are built, facilities for trade or business are severely limited and only a very small proportion of people can expect to be self-employed at any time. Sometimes a body of Africans are elected to consult with European municipal authorities on the running of the township but these bodies have little or no real executive powers and exist only to give a semblance of democracy.

Standards of accommodation vary enormously. In the days before the second world war there was little or no planning of African residential areas and houses were put up as the occasion demanded by governments, municipalities, private employers and by the Africans themselves. More recently some order has emerged and many of the derelict shanties built by the Africans out of corrugated iron, sacking and petrol tins hammered flat have been pulled down and replaced by properly-built houses.

Men predominate in the urban areas but it is not easy to say exactly what the proportion may be. In the older towns the number of women is fast catching up with the men but even in African townships such as Bulawayo or Salisbury it is unlikely that there is more than one woman to every dozen men. Most of the men are accommodated in bachelor-type houses, single rooms built either in rows or occasionally detached and large enough to accommodate four or five adults. Married accommodation varies from the same type of small rooms that are used for single men to three and four-roomed bungalows with running water in the kitchen and, very occasionally, lavatories incorporated into the house. Neither government, municipalities nor private employers have wholly good or wholly bad records as builders and owners of African accommodation. There is some excellent government-built accommodation and some that almost defies description. Thus, in their report on the causes leading up to the strike of African railway employees in 1945, the Tredgold Commission commented upon the accommodation available to railway employees, a Government responsibility, in the following words : —

'In its heyday, which was back in the early days of the century, the compound could not have been a particularly attractive residential proposition. For the most part, it consists of ill-lit and ill-ventilated barrack-type rows of rooms. Now 2,173 African men and women are housed in accommodation which officially should house 1,450. Latrine and bathing provision is inadequate. Save in one section of the compound there is no provision for cooking, which is done for the most part on home-made braziers in the open. Cooking in wet weather must be very difficult, men and women are crowded in rooms without regard to hygiene or decency. For example, we found 6 males, 3 females and 4 children occupying one room 15 foot × 17 foot 9 ins. × 11 foot 6 ins. in height. This was by no means exceptional. In an attempt to gain a little privacy, partitions of old sacking or rags are erected which further reduce light and ventilation. It is a miracle that no serious epidemic has originated here. If the present conditions in No. 2 compound are permitted to continue a day longer than can be avoided, it will be a lasting disgrace to the railway administration and to the government of this colony.'

It was not until early in the 1950's that all this railway accommodation was finally cleared away and replaced by more hygienic accommodation.

Housing built by the municipalities is very rarely better than the best government-built accommodation and usually a good deal worse. The situation in Bulawayo was devastatingly criticized in 1949 when Mr J. McNamee, an experienced native affairs administrator from South Africa undertook a survey of the urban situation on behalf of the municipality. One comment of his is particularly relevant: 'Some years ago,' he wrote, 'Sir Edgar Thornton, of the Union Department of Public Health, described certain areas situated immediately outside Port Elizabeth as "the worst slums in the world". He might well have qualified that statement had he seen the conditions of some of the shanty settlements in Bulawayo's industrial area.'

Typical of these was an instance where 135 men were excavating a quarry. When the quarry was first worked over twenty years before, the employers built sixty back-to-back single rooms for their African labourers, each measuring ten foot square. For years the owners of the compound had turned a blind eye to the gradual build-up of the compound population. Friends, children and relatives of both sexes were gradually incorporated into the small community and at the time of Mr McNamee's investigations there were, in addition to the 135 men at work on the quarry, 52 other men living in the compound and working elsewhere, 85 women and 73 children. To accommodate this surplus population a shanty community had grown up in the vicinity. Built, as are all shanties, of any available local material, these little homes provided a dismal picture. Pieces of corrugated iron formed the walls in most cases. The roof as a rule was made of petrol tins beaten flat, pieces of wood, rough plaster and sometimes sacking. Large stones were placed on most of these roofs to prevent them from blowing away.

Some of these little homes were completely detached. Others were built in groups, back-to-back or side-to-side. Some contained one room, others were divided into two or more. Some of them looked so small that it seemed impossible that they could contain more than one room, but it often turned out that they accommodated two or three families, a common door giving access to a narrow passage, down which the occupants crawled on hands and knees to little dens. When these shanties were divided into two or three rooms, somewhat more privacy was accorded to the occupants than could be obtained in the larger rooms built by the employers. So small, however, did these rooms become when divided, that their habitation by adults was something of a gymnastic feat. None of the shanties were of any standard size. Materials available, and needs of the individual builder determined the form that each took. Few of them exceeded

9 feet in length or 5 feet in height. In none was it possible to stand upright.

Typical of conditions in most similar areas, there was only one water point available for all the inhabitants of the compound and as this water was turned on for less than an hour each day, the squalor and the general dirtiness of the inhabitants added to the unpleasant odour in each smoken-laden and musty den. Perhaps the worst example of human degradation I encountered in all my visits to African townships was found in this compound. It was a shanty 5 feet 2 inches long, 6 feet wide and just over 4 feet high. In it lived a mad woman, her husband and two children aged approximately one and three years. The man was away working most of the day. His wife lay on the bare earth floor of her home, staring fixedly into space, while her two naked and filthy children crawled about amongst the cooking pots which were never washed because the woman could not move and the man was never home when the water was turned on. The shanty contained no piece of furniture, no box, not even a blanket. The wife lay on an old sack and she looked as grimy as the smoke-blackened walls of her home. Some help was given by friends, but it was spasmodic and unreliable. Flies, drawn into the house by the stale food, the sweat and the dirty pots, covered the woman and the children. The place cannot be adequately described in words. This particular little home was an exception. But the general conditions ruling in the compound itself were by no means unusual. Unfortunately the people who criticize the African mostly never venture into such places or see for themselves the background against which so many Africans eke out a precarious urban existence.

Public Health Acts variously lay down certain minimum standards. But these legislative measures were for the most part introduced before native administrators had come in contact with detribalized African family life and when Africans in employment were almost always single men who spent only a few months of the year in town. There are restrictions on back-to-back houses and regulations setting out the amount of window space and ventilation required per square or cubic foot. The amount of space per adult varies in different Bye-Laws between 250 and 500 cubic feet. But nowhere do the Bye-Laws recognize that adults may well not all be of the same sex and need privacy as much as they need ventilation.

In practice the regulations are largely ignored. Owing to the large influx of Africans into town they could not be complied with by private compound owners or even by the municipality and the Government. Industrial expansion would have been retarded by insisting upon the various provisions being enforced and eviction from insanitary quarters would, in the absence of alternative accommodation, have been too harsh.

For the present therefore the overriding impression given by a visit to the majority of urban areas is one of chronic overcrowding. This overcrowding hangs like a dark shadow over every facet of African life. It is in varying degrees to blame for most of the ills that beset the urban African. It takes two forms.

There is sheer numerical overcrowding by which is meant too many bodies, irrespective of sex or age, crowded into too small a space. To establish just how many people do actually occupy a single room or married accommodation is extremely difficult. Those who have no pass or authority to be there, and such people may well be in the majority, are unwilling to admit where they do live on being so questioned. Hence government or municipal authorized counts have little true value. Raids are sometimes carried out by police at night to check for what are termed 'loafers' and on such occasions quite startling overcrowding is disclosed. But not many rooms can be checked on any one night in this way as the news of the raid soon gets about. But not even day-time counts by people not connected with the law in any way can give a fair idea of the discomfort that must accompany living in these quarters. One such survey conducted by the author showed that many of the single men's rooms in one large African township, rooms that measured 10 feet by 11 feet, contained over six people and some even accommodated twelve.

The second form of overcrowding that is apparent is rather more social than arithmetical. A room that can accommodate five men without undue discomfort could be called overcrowded if it contained three men and a woman or girl. Allowing 250 cubic feet per person may not be palatial but if each of the individuals is of the same sex no great harm need arise. But where, as is in fact generally the case, there are women and children present as well, overcrowding takes on a more sinister form. People in Britain would know well enough what to expect in the way of delinquency were their children to grow up in close proximity to and with no privacy from several unmarried adults, one of whom would be their mother, and where the men living in the room took turn and turn about with the women present until they tired of them and sent them away with their children. Such human tragedies are found in almost every occupied room in most urban townships and locations and go far to explain the intransigence and the often vicious behaviour of young detribalized African men and women.

The blame for this overcrowding and for the many social ills that spring from it cannot be laid wholly upon the Europeans. They have built, at very great cost to themselves, enough houses for the number of Africans actually in employment. What they have not been able to do is to prevent the non-working or occasionally-working Africans from entering the townships and living there. Nor, of course, has any limitation been possible on the number of young Africans born to the women who have also entered the towns. What has happened is that towns have grown up, out of balance in most ways though they may be, where the Europeans intended only worker accommodation.

A drift to the towns is not something that is unique to Africa. In part it may spring from a lack of any positive policy for the rural areas, but every country that goes industrial must experience it in varying degrees. In Africa, however, there are certain features that aggravate the situation. The European towns represent progress and change. The African reserves are the past. To the older Africans there is very little incentive other than occasionally an economic motif, to learn something of the new way of life for which the towns stand. But to young Africans of both sexes, especially from tribal areas where traditional customs are breaking down, the towns exert a considerable pull. There is first and foremost freedom from irksome tribal discipline since tribal life still demands most of its old obligations and responsibilities. But on the other hand few of the privileges and the old excitements have survived the deadly hand of missionary and administrator. There is therefore none of the old balance that made it worth while accepting the traditional lore.

In the African townships there is very little adult discipline, there is a chance to learn more of the European way of life and to taste of the pleasures that white people are believed to enjoy in great measure. Money can be earned and education obtained, and these are the two factors that Africans believe have given Europeans their supremacy. In many cases, too, a journey to work in a distant town is demanded by prospective fathers-in-law. In olden times the young man had to show prowess in battle. Now that this opportunity is denied him following the forbidding of tribal raids, he can show his initiative in this more novel way. Many men go to town because erosion is reducing the potential of their agricultural holdings and when the menfolk leave for this reason the women are not slow to follow.

The proportion of women to men is increasing every year and since this goes to produce a more balanced population it must be welcomed. Unfortunately, the towns are still not organized to receive them. Apart from an occasional hostel for young girls there is virtually no accommodation available to them in which they can live with any pretext of decency or privacy. In almost every room or house these so-called single women can be found. In every case they are living in some kind of sexual relationship with one of the male occupants. In some cases the relationship lasts for a few hours. Sometimes it may last for weeks or even months and there are many cases where a man and woman have lived together in this way for many years.

This situation would appear to be general of the urban areas of Southern Africa. Writing of Broken Hill, in Northern Rhodesia, Geoffrey Wilson states : —

> 'the essentially temporary nature of the present situation is manifest in a certain blurring of the lines of distinction between different types of unions and different categories of woman. The distinctions we draw, in general terms, between prostitutes and concubines and between them and peripatetic, long-term and life-long wives are necessary for understanding, but they are often difficult to draw in particular cases. No woman, except the last, confine themselves to one category alone, and there is a constant tendency for one type of woman to pass gradually into another.'

Very few men coming into town for the first time trouble to ask the authorities for accommodation. For one thing they know well enough that there is none available. But this does not deter them greatly. Few of them do not have a brother, cousin or some relative to whom they can go for help.

The authorities naturally condemn this wholesale migration to the towns and the overcrowding that it imposes. But control is extremely difficult. A rigid pass system, imposed by an incorruptible police able to raid homes frequently by night and then expel all those found in illegal occupation, might, perhaps succeed for a time. But all too often following such a raid, the culprits are back again in a few days, happily re-occuping their old corner of a room confident in the knowledge that if caught again, there is every likelihood of the other occupants of the room clubbing together to pay whatever fine is imposed. Police measures of this kind are employed in South Africa and the results of imposing them are well enough known. The world condemns and the local Africans grow increasingly bitter, yet even in South Africa many elude the net. Women, for example, have for years successfully opposed the introduction of female pass laws and are still able to come and go almost as they please.

In Central Africa there is a half-hearted attempt to employ South African methods of control. Until passes and permits were very considerably reduced in 1961, a man could have had to carry as many as fourteen different documents. He required a pass for himself, one if his wife was in town (one for each wife) and yet another for his children. Visitors to his home required a pass to spend the night with him and other passes were needed to seek work or to be in the European part of the town. Many Africans found and are still finding it necessary to carry the receipt for the watch they wear or the parcel they carry as police are liable to stop and question them. Unlike Europeans, Indians and Coloureds, they were also obliged to

Bad Citizens

carry at all times a document in which is set out their full personal details, details of their employment and when they were last examined for venereal disease. The need to carry this variety of documents was much resented while the physical difficulty of coping with them was very considerable for people who could not read what was recorded on them or whose trouser pockets were, as was so often the case, in holes.

It is unlikely that passes were ever very effective in controlling African migration to the town or restricting the entry of men not prepared to work. Ways and means of obtaining both passes and accommodation are soon found. Bribery of African clerks can frequently obtain a married house for clever men with the necessary cash. Passes could be obtained in the same manner. Those without money usually have friends who will help. In the last resort black men will always help fellow black men to circumvent the white man's law. In any case, any system of control must lean heavily upon the integrity of its police and in Central Africa few, if any, of the local municipal police bodies have as yet built up any of the basic integrity that could make possible a sound disciplinary body. The McNamee Report spoke of one municipal police force in the following graphic words :

> 'For maintaining good order in the Bulawayo Location there is an establishment of seventeen municipal police boys. Judging by the appearance of these men, their physique, carriage, dress and general deportment, I should imagine that as far as controlling a location is concerned, they are a dead loss.'

While housing shortages exercise, perhaps, the most profound influence on the urban African, there can be little doubt that the extraordinary mixed nature of the urban population runs it a close second. When the first towns and mining camps were built they drew their labour largely from the local tribes. But this practice has changed completely. For one thing African men prefer to work farther away from their homes rather than nearby. Often they will make journeys of many hundreds of miles with the prime objective of being as far away from grasping relatives as possible. Other reasons for the change in the composition of urban populations are that local tribes alone cannot provide all the labour required and in many instances towns or mines have grown up in areas unoccupied by any tribe.

Today most urban areas contain an extraordinary diversity of tribal groups, of languages and even of ways of life. A dozen different languages may be spoken in a single street and there may be thirty or forty different tribes represented in the immediate vicinity. Very few accurate statistics showing the composition of urban or mining communities are available but it would be rare to find any area in which more than a quarter of its inhabitants derive from one tribe. The vast majority are alien to the area and even alien to the territory in which the town or mine is situated. For example, until the recently imposed ban on alien workers was introduced in Southern Rhodesia, there were more Africans of alien origin, that is from Northern Rhodesia, Nyasaland and Portuguese Africa employed in Salisbury and Bulawayo than there were Southern Rhodesia Africans, and the same is true though to a lesser degree for the whole territory.

The female population is almost exactly opposite in its national composition to the male. Three quarters of the African women living in any town will have come in from tribes in the immediate vicinity. And it is from these local women that African workers from distant tribes must find their urban wives. The result is a preponderance of inter-tribal marriage. These marriages are rarely marriages in the European sense of the term in that their degree of permanence is dictated almost entirely by the length of time the man remains in the town. Very few aliens take the women home whom they marry in the towns.

Increasingly the population of the towns is deriving more and more from the children of these inter-tribal marriages. Such children owe allegiance to no tribe. The language spoken by their mothers is the first they learn and they then pick up a smattering of English or some local lingua-franca that serves for most people in the particular area. Rarely do they learn the language of their father's tribe who in most cases will neither accept nor recognize them. Often the same situation pertains with the mother's tribe as well. Her marriage is usually looked upon as invalid and her children illegitimate since the husband is not as a rule in a position to conform with the various marriage laws practised by her tribe. For their part this lack of tribal interest in their welfare worries the children very little. Born and brought up in the towns they have no desire to leave. They see their futures in the urban areas and the greater opportunity that the towns offer as well as the lack of discipline both confirm them early in this view.

In the not too distant future young town-born children will be able to provide all the labour that is required and when that happens there will be far less diversity of tribe and language, and life will be a lot easier for the average man.

Even men and women who have succeeded in obtaining a house of their own and subsequently been able to keep most of the potential lodgers at bay, are still faced with many problems of adjustment. Europeans are prone to overlook the fact that the kind of house in which they themselves live and the layout of the neighbourhood in which it is situated both to a considerable extent derive from the

Bad Citizens 79

kind of family life that has grown up in Europe. In tribal society the layout of African homes was also related to their particular form of family life. Each woman would have her own hut, children would grow up in awe of their father, of whom they saw very little, and relations or in-laws would be accommodated near enough to be of help but not too near to interfere.

For these and other reasons too, it is extremely difficult for the average African family to settle down and easily adapt themselves to the kind of house and the town planning that the European administration, supposing them to be like Europeans, has provided for them.

A few examples may make this clear.

There is first the relationship of a man with his wife. European homes are peculiarly well adapted to the western concept of companionship in marriage. Married couples in western society have much in common. They have similar educational backgrounds, common interests, common tastes. By and large they find their happiness in each others company. This does not happen to anywhere near the same extent in Africa. Whereas in western society the sex of an individual is of little importance in so far as training and education go until that individual starts to work—and even then it matters less and less—in African society the activities and training of the sexes are different from the moment they can walk. The sexes receive quite distinct educations, they live separately, often eat separately and rarely play together. They may well make love together from a much earlier age than is common in the west but this is in keeping with the general pattern of tribal thinking. Men and women are quite distinct beings with their respective functions and attributes. Their only common interest lies in their biological interdependence and this becomes valid at puberty or even before. When a couple contracted a tribal marriage they generally married for life and it would be misleading to suggest that no measure of companionship was achieved between the two. Yet it was a different kind of companionship, a companionship based upon an agreed difference in function and responsibility. The wife, by tradition, never interfered in her husband's activities and he left his wife to her own duties. Both were sovereign in their own spheres and the group, rather than the family, ensured that responsibilities were honoured. As was shown in Chapter IV, no attempt was made to idealize sexual love in the way that has developed in western society over the past few hundred years, and endearments between husband and wife were neither expected nor desired.

To people brought up in such a tradition the difficulties of living together in one or possibly two small rooms must be considerable. Apart from their sexual interest in each other they have little else in common and no traditional motive to find an interest in each other's routine activities. In addition, both lack the companionship of closer relatives or friends from amongst their immediate neighbours whose presence, in tribal society, provided an antidote to boredom in the family home.

Urban wives have little to do from morning to night. Hot meals are something of a luxury for the majority and few families can afford more than one a day. Children's clothes can be more easily acquired than made and few women can pass the time reading as the vast majority are illiterate. They have their children to care for but when these are at school this activity is confined to only a limited period of the day. They are not, therefore, particularly stimulating companions for their husbands. In addition to their being rather dull there are also other factors mitigating against the development of companionship in marriage. Chief amongst these are overcrowded homes, of which no further comment is necessary, educational differences, poverty and the man's attitude towards his mother.

Very few men can hope to find wives of comparable educational levels to themselves. This situation will change as more girls go to school and remain in school through all the standards. At present, however, there is still a dearth of women of marriageable age with any educational qualifications.

The difference in experience and outlook is further evidenced in town where so very many more opportunities exist for men to widen their knowledge. Women tend to be the more conservative sex in African urban society and this further widens the gulf between a husband with his eyes on the future and a wife with her heart in the past. It is for this reason, no doubt amongst others as well, that has led to many educated Africans marrying European women when they come to Britain.

While it could be argued that poverty need not be a difficulty in a marriage between two people genuinely desiring to make their marriage a success, there is no doubt that when there is domestic trouble, some little luxury will smooth the wheels and go a long way to putting the relationship back on a proper footing. Most husbands can, however, only buy such little luxuries by severely cutting down on essentials such as food or clothing.

One of the African's most difficult hurdles in adapting to the European form of married life lies in the attitude towards his mother that tribal life has imprinted upon him. As a lad, all requests to his father were made through his mother, and she in her turn bestowed all the love and tenderness, that tradition prevented her from giving to her husband or receiving from him, upon her sons. The special relationship between a man and his mother continued after his marriage and he automatically put his mother's interests or wishes

Bad Citizens

before those of his wife. This attitude received the full support of tribal opinion and was in fact consistent with the African's whole attitude to blood relationships.

St Paul must have had primitive peoples and their marriage customs in mind, when he counselled on marriage 'Therefore shall a man leave his father and his mother and shall cleave unto his wife'. How right he may have been to have advised so revolutionary a change without first taking steps to prepare the social soil, is open to question. The same problem confronts administrators and missionaries at the present time.

A further difficulty is that the economic and social background of urban life tends to severely restrict the opportunities for husbands and wives to indulge in social activities together. They are very rarely seen dancing together, drinking beer together or watching sports together. Traditional separation of the sexes other than for biological purposes is one reason for this. In addition there is the old idea of non-participation in each others activities which results in many wives being wholly ignorant of what work their husband does or who employs him. Frequently wives do not know their husband's tribe or country of origin. As with many European wives, they are also often ignorant of how much he earns.

An essential practical difficulty that derives from the present rather than the past and that yet effectively prevents husband and wife going out together even should they feel so inclined is the problem of the younger children. In a normal urban community the neighbours can usually be counted upon to help in this matter. But in the African townships the neighbours are so often people of different language, culture and standards of behaviour that wives do not willingly entrust their children to them. The Matabele of Southern Rhodesia, for example, differ as much from, say the Senna people of Portuguese East Africa, as do the English from the Portuguese. Crêches for African children are often talked about by Europeans interested in African welfare but that is about as far as it goes.

When husbands and wives do go out together, perhaps for example when the family go to Church on Sundays, it is extremely rare to see them walk side by side in the European fashion. The husband usually walks along a little ahead followed by wife and children. The more sophisticated Africans can sometimes be seen walking side by side or even linking arms. They do this because they feel that it befits their European clothes and the European customs they attempt to copy. But they clearly do not enjoy the experience. They appear very self-conscious and ill-at-ease and as soon as they can they break apart and, on reaching Church, the men hurry over to join friends of their own sex and the women do the same.

The maintenance of polygamous marriages in urban homes raises obvious problems. It may be that on certain moral grounds there should be little sympathy for the polygamist in his problems. But this is not a very helpful attitude. Polygamy is a very old-established and in its way valuable custom. It ensured that there were no uncared-for women in a community where the hazards of life caused a severe shortage of men in the upper and middle age levels. As Dr Edwin Smith, an authority on the tribes of Central Africa has remarked, 'The surreptitious concubinage practised by large numbers of African Christians is worse than polygamy—it inflicts a greater wrong upon the women.' There are certainly grounds for ending this ancient practice now that social conditions are changing but it is still questionable whether life for a woman in a polygamous family is any worse, all things considered, than is a monogamous union in which the wife all too often has to resort to prostitution to obtain the bare necessities of life.

Polygamists who have more than one wife in town usually choose two wives of the same tribe—often of the same family—but not necessarily of the husband's own tribe. Usually the two wives have separate rooms in the house, although cases do occur where both women share the same room without any apparent trouble.

The majority of men with two wives are tending more and more to keep one or both of them at home in the reserves. In part this is due to economic forces and in part to ridicule. Wives in the country feed themselves and do not need so many clothes. A second wife in town, on the other hand, is an added expense on an already strained budget, and it is not of course always easy to provide her with a separate room as tribal custom and good psychology would demand. There is also the fear of infidelity and the derision with which both the polygamist and his wives are greeted by those of their neighbours who have accepted the Christian morality and who have come to think that polygamy is a mark of barbarity or primitive greed.

The kitchen presents a number of further problems to the African who is not used to the European type of house. Few families can afford the fuel to heat a living-room as well as the kitchen fire and therefore they crowd into the kitchen on cold nights. But for reasons that derive from tribal thinking, the less sophisticated Africans do not like to watch their wife cooking and the wife likes being watched even less. 'I feel that I am naked,' one woman remarked when she was asked why she did not like to cook while there were others in the room. Kitchen-living-rooms have thus no appeal to the average African. He prefers a small kitchen that leaves more space for the living-room but on cold nights when the smallness of the kitchen precludes the family sitting round the only fire they can afford, the only alternative to sitting in a cold room is to go to bed.

When the food is cooked it is customary for the father to eat apart, sometimes joined by his elder sons. Up to a point this is still largely practised but when the husband is separated from his wife and children merely by the floor space of a small room, he does not feel that his position in the family is receiving adequate recognition. There is nothing that he can do about it, but he does not like it.

Both these prejudices are largely based upon convention and given time they can be expected to disappear. The young people growing up in urban homes know that European parents eat with their children and they would like to do the same. This European practice is found already in a few of the more sophisticated homes and no doubt in time it will become general.

Parents-in-law create yet another problem. In every African tribe custom decrees that parents-in-law should be treated with considerable respect. In addition the son- or daughter-in-law must avoid them whenever they can. They may not cross their path, look them in the face or watch them sleeping or eating.

The African tribal homes made the maintenance of these avoidances comparatively simple. Each person had their own hut and it was easy enough to build a new hut in the event of the parents-in-law coming to stay. In the European type of urban house, the avoidances are no longer possible because each family must make the best use they can of one, two or three-roomed houses all under a single roof.

The motives that prompted this particular form of behaviour to a parent-in-law together with the significance and the meaning of the practice, have all largely vanished with the breakdown of the tribal system and consequently the sentiments associated with avoidances have today deteriorated to the level of vague superstitions. Nevertheless, they are still felt strongly, possibly even stronger than any other of the various superstitions and beliefs that are relics of olden days. Even the more cultured Africans still feel distinctly uncomfortable if they are obliged to eat in the same room with their wife's parents. Every effort is therefore made to maintain the avoidances. Sometimes small shanties are illegally built behind the house. Wherever possible, the parent-in-law stays with some other relative, but if no such person can be found the husband or wife frequently move into a neighbour's home for the duration of the visit. Occasionally two neighbours have an arrangement whereby each accommodates the others parents-in-law.

The urban type of home makes it particularly difficult to follow tribal custom in the event of a death occurring in the family. In almost every tribe some sort of action is taken with regard to the house of the dead man. In some cases the house is completely destroyed, sometimes it is deserted for a prescribed period and in certain tribes the members of the family continue in occupation only after the local witch doctor has purified it of all association with death. Certain Nyasa tribes run up against a particular difficulty. It is their practice to bury children who die before cutting their first teeth beneath the hearth of the family home. The idea behind this is that the soul of the dead child must be given a second chance and it is felt that if placed just beneath the floor it is in a particularly advantageous position to be reborn to the wife at her next confinement. It is not only the municipal authorities who object to the maintenance of this custom. African neighbours object just as strongly.

European-type houses are not designed for customs of this kind or indeed for destruction whenever somebody dies. Nor are the authorities disposed to allow occupants to change their house on the death of a member of the family. Even where African witch doctors can be found to carry out the necessary ritual of purification there are difficulties associated with the rites because the necessary ingredients are seldom to hand and the beer that is essential if the goodwill of the ancestral spirits is to be gained cannot be acquired.

Despite these many and often unfamiliar difficulties, Africans nonetheless are, circumstances permitting, as house-proud as any other people. It is quite startling sometimes when surveying the long line of drab exteriors to walk inside, sometimes in the case of shanties to crawl inside, and find there order, cleanliness and indeed a certain style.

But these are individual instances and do not appear to represent a common desire. No one area or street of any town ever stands out in this respect above another. In part this derives from the custom of allocating houses to the man at the top of the waiting list. As a result of this system every street contains every sort and condition of men. Recently in some of the more far-sighted municipalities and mining towns attempts have been made to segregate what are termed the 'emerging African middle class' but these attempts are usually only half-hearted and rarely achieve their object since it is the middle-classiness of the man that is considered and not his wife. She finds adjustment even more difficult than does her husband and as it costs much money for the African man to maintain the outward trapping of his middle class, his home and his wife are often less well cared-for than are those of relatively poorer but classless Africans.

The cost of starting a new home is very considerable and new or even secondhand furniture is something of a luxury. Consequently few Africans possess what Europeans would call the necessary minimum. Most families acquire furniture piece by piece over a long period and their homes therefore reflect a very varied pattern. Some houses contain nothing but a few blankets and cooking pots. Others are equally bare of necessities but contain a sewing machine or a gramophone in solitary splendour in the living-room. Usually the living-room is furnished before the bedrooms and only in very few houses are all the rooms well furnished.

A very real problem, both to the Africans themselves as well as to the authorities, is the matter of leisure. African workers differ in one significant respect from the workers in Britain during the Industrial Revolution, with whom they are frequently compared, in that they do, in fact, have a considerable amount of spare time. Many concerns stop work at four o'clock and almost all Africans who are not on shift work have finished work by five o'clock in the afternoon. In addition, many employers are adopting the five-day week and therefore the whole of Saturday and Sunday are free for whatever form of recreation the individual may choose.

In England and in other industrialized countries, leisure time pursuits and the provision made for them have evolved gradually as working hours have decreased. In Central Africa the labourer enters industry when the hours are already drastically reduced.

The result of this is that the African, removed from his traditional environment, does not know how to pass his spare time and his white masters have little idea how he should and they are reluctant to spend too much money on the provision of leisure-time pursuits that may well be unsuitable.

There are limited opportunities for young people, especially for boys, to play various games. Football is the most popular and there is a little tennis, boxing, cycle racing and netball. People who do not play games because they are either disinterested or too old have little official help in finding relaxation. Some towns have cinemas but the quality of the films, almost always cowboy epics, is very poor and the plot is difficult to follow since the films themselves are heavily cut. Africans are not supposed to see Europeans behaving in a manner likely to bring a white skin into disrepute and this tends to eliminate most of the plot. Cartoons, however, are shown right through without a cut and are about the highest level of intellectual opportunity available in the cinema.

Ballroom dancing is very popular. Yet despite the European form of the music and many of the mannerisms including even the wearing of white tie and tails, the dance itself remains essentially African. And as in tribal life it is a man's activity. The best of the dancers give a quite remarkable performance of skill and agility. They dance with women more, it would seem, for form's sake than for preference. They are equally as happy dancing alone or with another man. And when a man and woman finish dancing it is the woman who wipes the sweat from her face not, as in the western world, the man.

Indoor games have not really caught on to any extent. Actually the term 'indoor games' is used in its European sense since most indoor games are played by Africans in the open. Here it is cooler, it is traditional, and in the case of the particular game being illegal, it is easier to detect the arrival of the police and so disperse with less chance of capture.

The most common game is 'Tsolo'. Variants of this game are found all over Southern Africa. It is not unlike draughts and the object is to take the opponent's men. Stones are placed in holes, there being four lines of holes and any number of holes in a line. It is not a difficult game and the speed with which the Africans make their moves betokens practice rather than brainpower. Both men and women play, though it is extremely rare to see a man and a woman playing against each other.

Card games are growing in popularity with the men, and in every case they are played for money although gambling is usually illegal. It does not seem from remarks passed by husbands and wives that gambling is attended with so many of the social evils that characterize it in other lands. Many wives complain that their husbands waste money in the beer hall or on other women but none ever mention gambling as a source of friction in the home.

Opportunities for reading are limited. In the first place the majority of people are illiterate. Then, too, electric light is installed in only a limited number of houses and these are not necessarily allocated to people with some education. Few homes have any books on show other than the Bible but most towns have lending libraries. In the main these are filled with volumes thrown out by Europeans seeking space on their own shelves and the Victorian type of novel seems generally to predominate.

Probably the most popular forms of relaxation are drinking and sex. Africans are heavy drinkers by tradition. But drinking in the tribal areas was kept within certain defined bounds. There was a certain amount of light-hearted drunkenness, 'beer before the eyes' as it was called, but rarely did it lead to anti-social behaviour. For one thing the beer that was brewed was more of a food than a drink and did not have a very high alcoholic content. For another there were strong forces of public opinion and tradition that prescribed when one might drink heavily and what might and might not be done when one had. Most drinking was associated with some ceremonial or other but as there were plenty of these the opportunities for revelry were many. The Matabele of Southern Rhodesia have a proverb that runs, 'The stomach being boneless is capable of infinite expansion', and most tribes subscribed to this belief in their drinking habits. Where Europeans drink in pints the African drinks in gallons.

Beer drinking in towns differs fundamentally from beer drinking in the tribal reserves. The special form of beer usually favoured by ancestral spirits, should a man wish to propitiate them, is not available and there are a number of European-imposed restrictions. Beer can only be drunk in somewhat sordid beer halls and at certain hours of the day, drunkenness itself is an offence, people may not brew their own beer nor drink it in their homes, and they could not, until very recently, obtain European-type beer, wines or spirits on the grounds that they were said to be incapable of holding their liquor.

The result of these restrictions upon a people who traditionally enjoyed drinking as much for social reasons as any other, was inevitable. A great deal of illegal brewing grew up in every township. The traditional African type of beer, 'Kaffir Beer' as it is called, is relatively easy to make but it requires some five or six days to ferment and during this time it can be easily detected by reason of the strong fumes it puts off. Making it is therefore a somewhat hazardous occupation. An alternative is a drink known as 'skokiaan' that is distilled from a number of highly intoxicating and often poisonous substances but as it can be drunk a day after manufacture it is safer to brew. The basis of this 'skokiaan' is usually corn or potatoes with a little European spirit and any agent such as carbide, boot polish or other similar product that will give it a venomous kick. A pint of it is more than most men can take and the poisonous effect it has on their stomachs must be considerable. There is, too, a considerable black market in European spirits such as whisky, gin and rum.

Illegal brewing is usually practised by the women and provides them with an additional source of income. Most of them combine brewing with a little prostitution for good measure. Some of the more enterprising Africans operate mobile brothels, mobile because of the danger of police detection, wherein they offer to weekend customers as much drink and women as they care to have for a pound. The organizers of these unusual forms of entertainment do extremely well on the deal. Men come in on Friday evening and are given a pint of skokiaan. This puts them to sleep till well into Saturday evening. None too well when they wake up, the tougher members essay a little beer and only very few of them demand one of the lady brewers in accordance with the terms of the agreement. Much Monday morning absenteeism derives from such weekends.

In some towns and on some private compounds individual workers with a long record of service are allowed to brew beer at the weekend. They take this in turn and the lucky men can make anything up to £50 in the process. Incentives of this kind are much more effective in holding labour than are offers of somewhat small weekly pensions after twenty or more years service. The understanding employer or compound managers are as aware of this as are the Africans themselves but of course such practices can never be quoted during discussions on how labour turnover can be reduced.

Sex is the African's other major form of relaxation. Boredom, the relative scarcity of women, the generally unsatisfactory conditions of life must all be variously responsible for the degree of sexual activity and the enormously high rate of venereal disease. Prostitution flourishes in almost every African town or compound. In the larger towns the prostitutes are residents themselves. On smaller mining towns they sometimes hire buses and go round from mine to mine arranging their itinerary to match pay-day on each mine. There have been cases where the women have written asking the mines to change their pay-day as it clashed with another nearby.

The African probably takes to an easy sex life more readily than does a European as he is not encumbered in the course of his upbringing by any puritanical beliefs or concepts. Certain tribes valued virginity in brides but as most women were married at puberty there were few transgressors. Western civilization keeps its children at school long after puberty and at the same time holds back sexual activity by a series of taboos, conventions, and various sanctions that are both supernatural and legal. Few of these can apply to first or second generation detribalized Africans and the majority of them start their sex life when nature intended that they should. A high proportion of girls in the higher forms have to leave school because they are pregnant—though rarely to boys from the same school—and prostitutes report that boys are frequent customers.

The general health of the urban African populations is low but it is not easy to obtain comparative figures. The health services themselves are good and become better every year but good health must depend more upon the conditions of living than upon curative facilities. The conditions of living have to some extent already been described. The average African is unable to obtain sufficient of the essential foods and his mental health suffers because of the frustration he encounters on every side as he tries, at least for a time, to improve his standard of living. An important element in the health of any population is sanitation and in the case of the urban African this is either inadequate or, in some townships, totally non-existent.

It is possible to compare the causes of death in African and European populations living in close proximity to each other. These show that where a disease carries off more Africans than Europeans it is due to a variety of factors of which congested accommodation, incorrect feeding, the lack of immunity to the diseases of western civilization, and the debilitating effect of the various worm diseases—to which Europeans are not usually prone—are all variously responsible. Where the European death rate tends to exceed the African it is due principally to the greater longevity of the Europeans that renders them more liable to the diseases of the aged.

The greatest present scourges to the Africans are tuberculosis and venereal disease. The former is very difficult to treat because of the risks of infection or re-infection in overcrowded homes and the general low level of nutrition. Venereal disease is rife amongst all sections of the population and many Africans have been re-infected again and again. In one municipality it was found that 40 per cent of the men had suffered at one time or another and over 4 per cent of the children at school were congenitally syphilitic. Nor is the disease restricted to the less well-advanced section of the African community. The chairman of the Methodist Church in Southern Rhodesia said in 1950 that over 30 per cent of his ministers and teachers had suffered from venereal disease at one time or another.

Most Africans look upon gonorrhea as little more than an annoying irritant and it is only when they become infected with syphilis as well that they go for treatment. This is provided free and costs the authorities many hundreds of thousands of pounds in medicines alone. This money could be so much better spent, for the cost of giving penicillin to two patients would pay a year's fees, food and accommodation for an African boy or girl at school. But while conditions remain as they are it is unlikely that there will be any real improvement.

One of the African's problems is that he does not like the European type of hospital. He has nothing against the treatment he receives and he respects the skill of European doctors—in fact he has come to look on the injection with as much confidence as the neurotic European accords to unpleasant-tasting medicine—but hospitals are places he avoids if he possibly can. This springs principally from his attitude to death and his aversion to entering a house or room in which people have died.

When a man brought up in such a system of belief enters hospital, he is not only obliged to remain in a ward in which men die almost daily, but he even has to lie on a bed and in blankets in which others before him have passed away.

Even African priests with theological training and ordained into the Christian Church, people who should certainly be freer than most from superstition, feel strongly on this point. One stated that he did not care to visit people in hospital, let alone go there when he himself was ill, because, as he put it, 'The house is heavy'. Another admitted the efficiency of European medicine but only as a last resort. 'Hospital is like gaol. Nobody likes to go there, but when you have to go, you have to go.'

The African woman's readiness to go to the maternity clinic to have her baby is often referred to as a case where modern science has won over primitive superstition. In reality, it is nothing of the sort. The majority of women go to the clinic because only by doing so can they keep out of sight of their husbands for the requisite number of days that tribal custom demands.

Formal education is growing in every African town but the young men or women still learn more from the environment in which they live than from any schooling they may receive. The overcrowded homes, the poverty, the instability of marriage, the absence of family life, the lack of any active public opinion together with the low general level of morality, and of sexual morality in particular, all exercise a powerful educational influence. Reference has already been made elsewhere to the extent of these various forces and no further comment need be made on them in the present context. Their influence both directly and indirectly upon the growing child cannot be exaggerated.

The African parent cannot pass on very much good advice on how to live in a detribalized environment and this places his children at a serious disadvantage. As George Kennan, the American diplomat, once observed, 'Wherever the past ceases to be the great and reliable reference book of human problems; wherever, above all the experience of the father becomes irrelevant to the trials and searchings of the son—there the foundations of man's inner health and stability begin to crumble. These, unfortunately, are the marks of an era of rapid technological and social change.'

The tribal traditions of the parents are quite unsuited to the child in the strange new environment, while their inchoate way of life and unstable relationships unfit the vast majority for the tasks of educating young children at all. In many cases the children understand better than do their parents the strange new forces of western materialism though these children lack any of the stability that their parents acquired when growing up under the restraints of tribal discipline.

Schooling is provided by both government and missions and is usually free. Its benefits are, however, somewhat limited. Many children do not start school until they are in their teens. Parents are still often reluctant to send their daughters to school and the general instability of urban life makes for frequent changes of school for many children.

The curriculum in the primary schools poses further problems. Children have to learn to read in English, they are given religious instruction, drill, nature study, hygiene, history, geography and industrial work. The subjects are perhaps a little more varied than occur in European primary schools but the purpose of the curriculum is to bring them as far as possible to the academic level of a European child of twelve. There are still so few secondary schools as to make comment upon the contributions they make to African education unnecessary.

While the majority of Europeans dislike the African with some education and tend to ridicule his limited achievements, the urban Africans, almost to a man, take a very different view of those of their number who have acquired a little schooling, and they exaggerate out of all proportion the significance of the achievement.

It is very necessary to understand why this diversity of opinion exists and what are its causes. Although a great deal of the European condemnation of the educated African and of the system that has produced him is due to unreasoning race prejudices, there is no doubt that many of these Africans are all that their worst critics say of them. Many of them are lazy, many want everything for nothing and much that is learned at school is forgotten or ignored as soon as they leave.

Yet, neither for the faults of the African nor for his blind faith in the importance of Standard VI education can the curriculum or the educational system itself be blamed. Both are directly the product of social forces at work within the whole framework of urban life. When the Europeans criticize the produce of the African school or the school system itself, they are ignorant of the strength of the environmental influences and they fail to understand the purpose and the function of education. Neither missionary nor government schools can honestly be held responsible for the behaviour of those whose primary education has been cut short after two or three years, or for those who do not start their schooling until after puberty.

It is only by those who complete their schooling by the age of 13 that African schooling can honestly be judged. And who, when condemning the system, has ever based his observations or his criticism on this tiny sample? Even if such a study were to be made, and if it were found that these few pupils were dishonest, lazy, unreliable and so on, the blame could still not be levied on the schools. They hold the children's attention for less than thirty hours a week, and this is quite insufficient for even the most competent master to exert any real or lasting influence on the minds or spirits of young people, the majority of whose life is spent in the sordid atmosphere of compounds or location, children who have more opportunities of learning from the bad example of Europeans than they do from priests or schoolmasters.

By the time that most of the pupils arrive at school their characters have been largely formed. This is one of the drawbacks of having to impose a primary school curriculum designed in so far as its moral teaching is concerned, for children aged from six to twelve, upon a group of adolescents, of secondary school age or even higher, who have largely grown up in an environment that teaches little that is good. In normal conditions the authorities look to the parents at home to provide much of the character training and the basis of discipline. But as has already been shown, the urban African parents who are deprived of their traditional mode of instruction and who do not understand the new environment, are seldom competent to give the necessary training. They fully believe that it is provided in the schools.

The tendency of so many Africans, who have lived for some time under European influences, to expect something for nothing—a frequent subject of European criticism—cannot be denied. It springs, however, from too little education rather than from too much. As things are now, a young man or woman on leaving school knows about as much of the world, its government and its methods of administration as an English schoolboy of twelve. These Africans have only completed, and often under considerable difficulty, a primary school course. They know nothing of government, how it functions and whence it derives its funds; nothing of economics or any of the means whereby national effort is directed into active channels. They are taught no civics. How far such courses could be added to an already full curriculum is hard to say. But because they do not know about such things, they naturally hold the view that government possesses a bottomless purse into which it can dip whenever it feels the need. They know nothing of how Europeans live— save that they all seem fabulously rich—how they put by money for the future and how they are dependent upon wages and work for their whole well-being.

This attitude of expecting everything for nothing cannot be corrected in its educational context alone. It is closely tied up with traditional attitudes towards the ownership of wealth and the distribution of services. It is to some extent due also to official policy that has for so long denied the African any responsibility in the management of his own affairs. It is further due to a dictum inherent in the African's whole attitude to life, summed up in the Matabele proverb, 'The child that does not cry dies in his mother's carrying skin'.

In this highly complex and in many ways tragic situation the churches are of very little help. Their resources in both men and money are totally inadequate and their policy of spreading their staffs over wide areas, rather than concentrating them, is in many ways a drawback. Seldom, for example, can a European priest devote his full time to an urban community. As a rule he will be responsible for hundreds of square miles of territory with African villages scattered at long distances from each other. In many cases, too, he will also be responsible for the church schools in each village and community. All this travelling and supervision occupies more time than pastoral work itself.

As a result much of the day-to-day contact with church members and the giving of Communion is left to ordained African priests. Each denomination has its own ideas and techniques for training these African clergy. Occasionally a denomination will insist that an African priest should have the same qualifications as a European.

There are consequently very few such African priests. Other denominations demand a minimum Standard VI (primary schooling only) education and two or three years theological training thereafter with or without voluntary church work for a period of time. Other denominations again lay very little stress on education or theological training at all. In their view a man cannot expect to understand and sympathize with his flock until he has himself experienced and overcome the temptations to which they are liable. These denominations maintain that in urban work moral stamina and common sense are more important qualifications than those gained in the sheltered atmosphere of the missionary training school.

In practice the theological training that Africans receive gives only a thin veneer of Christian belief. Much of the old African religious thinking still survives, just as no doubt ancient Britons, converted to Christianity and enrolled as priests, still retained for a generation or two many of their traditional beliefs. Although guarded in their comments on such subjects as witchcraft, theologically-trained Africans are rarely willing to help a man believed to have been cursed by a witch. Some will claim that they might pray for a bewitched man but most would absolve themselves from interference in this tricky field by praying that the afflicted man might think rightly.

Most African priests, whether trained or not, see much similarity between Christian and primitive African belief. They explain that both tribal religion and Christianity believe in a life beyond the grave. Europeans, it is suggested, attain immortality through the Father and the African does so through his Son. But both reach whatever one cares to call Heaven. The rôle of the African ancestor in carrying the wishes of the living to God is similar to the Christian teaching of the rôle of Jesus Christ. They see the Catholic practice of praying to the Virgin Mary to intercede on man's behalf as but a variant of the African family system wherein the mother acted as intermediary to the father.

Few church buildings in African townships offer very much in the way of a refuge from the ugly turmoil outside. The general state of cleanliness, order and repair of most of these churches is deplorable. In part this is due to their daily use as school premises, but the full blame cannot by any means be placed upon the children and the teaching staff. Ink stains on the floors, dirty marks on the walls, half-cleaned blackboards and forms left untidily piled together are certainly the legacy of the daily class and they go far to make the atmosphere of almost every church so sordid. But the lack of paint, the poor state of the brickwork, the broken windows, the absence of electric light bulbs or lampshades is the responsibility of the European and African staff of the missions themselves.

Very often children attending school in the mission church are not allowed to use the mission lavatories and so, with public lavatories often some distance away they use the rubber hedges or fences surrounding each church. Nor are such habits restricted to the children. On Sunday afternoons, men can also be seen disappearing behind the churches for the same purpose. In the hot weather the odour of open-air sanitation around the entrance to many mission churches is appalling.

Sometimes too the African priests and their friends sleep in the vestry of their churches. These vestries, into which passers-by can look, are often full of women and children and unmade beds and closely resemble the overcrowded rooms of the town itself.

It is in such an atmosphere that those who come to church for meditation and prayer must find what comfort they can. The best that can be said about many of these churches is that they do not offer too great a contrast from the conditions in which the majority of the congregation live. There are, of course, exceptions, but they are few and far between. In these few instances, the churches do succeed in retaining some semblance of sanctity. They are churches uses as schools rather than schools used as churches.

In his rural home, the African Christian has usually known of only one Christian denomination even if he himself had not been an ardent supporter. He has usually heard of, and he may even have seen, the missionaries of other denominations to his own. But he has never experienced the diversity of ritual and belief that characterizes Christianity in its urban setting. In Bulawayo, for example, he finds some fourteen different denominations, all of whom offer him life everlasting if he abides by their rules, rules that may well be quite happily broken by members of the church gathering next door. Some denominations say he must not drink or smoke, others say he may not eat pork. Some forbid him to read the Bible altogether and others deny him only certain sections. Some say he may do no work on Saturdays. Polygamy is looked on with compassion in some denominations and rigorously condemned in others. To whatever denomination he gives his loyalty, he soon finds himself separated from fellow Christians by a diversity of practice and belief that is in its way as great as were the tribal differences of other days. To a considerable extent denominationalism amongst Christian Africans has replaced tribalism.

It is not easy to say how far religion satisfies or meets the need of the ordinary man and woman. The great work that the missionaries performed in the early days has left a legacy and a degree of loyalty which will take years of less personal contact to undo. There can be few African families who have not a profound reason for gratitude to some missionary in the rural areas. Medical aid, material assistance and encouragement were given freely. But today all this has changed. The missionary is a little-known figure, an administrator

Bad Citizens 95

rather than a priest or minister. And often his attitude towards the colour bar differs very little from that of other Europeans.

Such is the soul-destroying environment in which so many Africans are born and grow to maturity. There are problems of survival and adjustment of which the European settlers have no inkling. There is poverty, viciousness and boredom. There is little help and only frustration for those who attempt to better themselves. These various disabilities bear hard upon the men but for the women the situation is even more desperate. The town is a jungle and its terrors are infinitely worse than these women or their mothers ever knew in tribal days. They can find no worthwhile employment, no privacy and no security in marriage. There is indeed much truth in the suggestion that Europe's greatest contribution to the confusion of Africa has been the single woman. Nor is their plight an individual tragedy, for it is they who are primarily responsible for bringing up the young Africans of the next generation.

Africans may well be bad citizens. It would be surprising if they were anything else.

CHAPTER 6

And Bad Workers

Men of all races work only to achieve some end. If that end is unattainable, or not valued very highly, they either work light-heartedly or not at all. The African in town is in just such a position. Only in isolated instances does he work to the full satisfaction of his European masters and, as a general rule, government officials and industrial, mining and commercial employers are unanimous in their condemnation of his inefficiency. Many of these opinions are founded upon prejudice or ignorance; yet there is, nonetheless, ample evidence in the form of high absentee rates, rapid labour turnover and an almost complete failure of normal incentives to produce increased productivity, to indicate that something is radically wrong.[1]

It is, perhaps, in the economic field that the African meets his greatest problems of adjustment. He has, of course, known and used money in the tribal areas for many years. Indeed he has for long valued it and sought to increase his store of it. But when he enters the towns he suddenly finds himself in a world in which money counts above all else, in which it is economic forces and not social forces that motivates the society in which he comes to live. People are seen to be fortunate or unfortunate, they have power or no power, status or no status, depending primarily upon the amount of money that they earn or that they possess. If they have insufficient for their needs they starve.

All this is the antithesis of what happens in tribal life and its effect on the African who meets it for the first time is very considerable. If at the start of his urban career and even for a generation or so later he is an indifferent disciple of the industrial order of the western world he has many excuses for his behaviour. All his traditions are against him, there is a history of ill-treatment at work going back some centuries, social conditions are not conducive to good work in themselves, there are economic forces as well as political forces to hinder his easy transformation. All these must be considered before a judgement is made and in setting them out it has to be recognized that some factors apply to a relatively small number of Africans, others may apply to the majority.

Although urbanization may not have started until comparatively recently, there are many Africans whose tribes have had long associations with European employers of one kind or another. Few of these

[1] Many of these criticisms apply equally to European workers but this fact is tacitly ignored.

early contacts were happy ones and two historical factors that still exert some influence in the Africans' thinking on the subject of work are slavery and the activities of labour recruiters.

It has been suggested that when slavery was abolished the African ceased to be an effective worker. The argument goes that both European employer and the African labourer are still, in varying degrees and in their own distinctive ways, influenced by the mentality that it engendered in both sections of the community. Freed slaves generally proved irresponsible, were reluctant to work hard unless closely supervised and, no longer having a universal provider, they tended to sink lower and lower in social squalor. According to Orde-Brown, much of the prevailing European attitude to native labour can also be traced back to the old days when slavery was almost universal in Africa.[1] At that time the master had the same feeling of proprietorship for his slaves as he had for his dogs or his cattle. They were his property and he wanted them to give of their best. Though there were bad slave-owners, it would appear that such were the exception. A man who did not look after his slaves failed for the same reason that a farmer who does not look after his cattle fails today. Slaves were, however, plentiful and so output per man was never high. Both master and slave, therefore, grew used to a rate of output that could never be tolerated in a wage-paying society in which employees have to support themselves on their own earnings. Today the slave-owner has gone and with him has vanished almost completely the sense of responsibility that he had for his workers. Unhappily, the slave-driving mentality has tended to outlive the practice of keeping slaves.

Following the abolition of slavery, labour recruiters were quick upon the scene. There were many more bad ones than good, despite the conditions that most of the African territorial governments attempted to impose so as to limit exploitation of one kind or another. Few tribes escaped the attentions of these men and the early history of the movement abounds with instances of false promises to native labourers and future employers alike. Often the conditions of employment and the nature of the contract were so ill explained that the effect upon the illiterate and simple tribesmen was the same as if they had been deliberately cheated. Some of the consequences of this dishonesty can still be discerned in the suspicion and disillusionment that underlies labour relations in Central Africa today.

Even before the African reaches his urban destination his attitude to working is to some extent already formed by the reasons prompting him to leave home in the first place. These reasons are many and varied and differ profoundly from those found in Western Europe

[1] See Orde-Browne, G. St. J. *The African Labourer*. (Oxford University Press 1933).

where a drift to the towns is a commonplace event. Many of the reasons given for migrating to town or mine have already been discussed. But the one reason for which Africans do not come to town is specifically to work. This is something his European employer almost always fails to recognize and it is this fact more than most that makes the African's response to the type of incentives that prompt a European to work harder almost negligible. Where, for example, the individual has come for the express purpose of acquiring certain possessions—a bicycle or a suit of clothes—no promises of increased money for extra work will achieve any overall increase in production because the individual merely leaves for home rather sooner than he would normally have done. Most Africans do their best to obtain whatever article they hoped to acquire; but all too often the amount of work required or the degree of saving necessary is beyond their patience or ability. When this happens they lose all definite reason for remaining in town. Few of them return home, however, because of an unwillingness to admit failure or for fear of ridicule. Such men, and there are many such, find that the lack of any social sanctions and the atmosphere of living for the day that hangs so heavily over the urban scene, fits in better with their general lack of purpose in life than does the much closer discipline and strong public opinion still found in most tribal areas. And so they remain in town to swell the ever growing number of discontented, apathetic men whose sole pleasure in life is achieved by giving way to every momentary impulse.

Environmental factors must also play an important part—if not in actually shaping a man's attitude to work—then at least in rendering him less able to undertake his duties satisfactorily. Purely physical conditions, overcrowding, inadequate sanitation or recreational facilities, malnutrition or ill-health, exact a heavy toll of vital energy. Psychological factors are also operative. The whole conception of African urban life as seen by the European administrators is well expressed—both in its architecture and also in the legislation that is imposed—as the provision of boxes for machines or stables for draught horses. Much of the single men's accommodation does in fact closely resemble the kind of stabling found in the less well-to-do farms of Europe. That industrial efficiency must derive to a major extent from the type of homes in which the workers live is recognized by isolated government departments or responsible individuals. Thus, in his report for the year 1948, the Commissioner for Native Labour wrote of conditions that have only since marginally improved:

'What can be expected of those who exchange the fullness of tribal life with its innumerable social activities for the squalid, sordid surroundings of an overcrowded, filthy and verminous barrack or a tin shanty at the brickfields?'

In the same vein, living conditions in the shanty communities surrounding Bulawayo were described the following year by Mr McNamee in the course of his investigations on behalf of the city council. He wrote:

> 'Labour drawn from these settlements cannot possibly be efficient and living under such conditions must unquestionably be a factor in the creation of a spirit of hopelessness, sullenness and desperation. And this spirit can early develop into mass disaffection.'

Actual conditions at work vary enormously. In a few factories and on some of the larger mines conditions compare favourably with anything found in Europe. But the existing factory laws and the legislation relating to feeding and payment of workers are limited in their application because of a lack of adequate governmental inspection.

This inadequacy was summed-up to me by one of the government native labour department inspectors who, when I asked him why he did not visit certain factories where labour policy was generally known to be contrary to the law, replied, 'What is the use while the Government is composed of business men? If we make trouble there are questions asked in Parliament and we get a rap over the knuckles.'

Good conditions and protective legislation even if they can be enforced are still of little use if the level of face to face supervision is indifferent or downright bad. Such is indeed the case. All matters relating to African welfare and conditions of service are usually left in the hands of some lowly-paid individual whose sole qualifications for the task are either long and usually undistinguished residence in Africa coupled with a knowledge of invective in a native tongue. Many of these men are ex-policemen, usually of South African descent. Typical was one man who had been for many years in charge of some 900 Africans in one of the smaller towns. I had asked him about the position of the more advanced African and in the answer that he gave and the illustration that he used he typified so many of his kind. These advanced Africans, he explained, liked nothing better than to imitate the customs of the Europeans when they were being watched by their less fortunate fellows. One of their practices was to hold 'Sundowner parties' in the local beer hall. For these functions, he said, they sat drinking their beer round a large table upon which had been placed a tablecloth and flowers. As the man described these unusual additions to the beer hall he was spluttering with fury and he finished the account with the remark, 'And I ask you, did God make flowers for Africans to put on their tables?'

As recently as the 1950's the majority of firms were unable to provide any personal details about their African labour force. The country of origin of the men and indeed often their length of service with the individual firm could only be obtained by examining the African's own registration cards. Nothing in the company records could provide this information. Irregularities in payment were also widespread, irregularities that sprung from the rudimentary time-keeping records and the ease with which those responsible for the African labour force could erase or change details of a man's pay. The low calibre of so many of those charged with the responsibility for African staffs was such as to make malpractice widespread. In certain instances even the managers of companies admitted that there were names of non-existent Africans added to the weekly or monthly pay lists. The reason given for this practice of recording 'ghosts' as they were called was explained by one senior executive as due to the need to obtain extra money out of the salary cheque to pay European apprentices. It appeared that these youths were in such short supply that the only way to recruit them was to offer them more pay than the apprentice agreement permitted. This extra money was obtained by the addition of the non-existent Africans to the wage lists.

Towards the end of the 1950's a number of firms and the larger mining companies began to introduce a better type of supervisor for their African staffs and to these individuals were often given the title of personnel manager. Record-keeping certainly improved and many of the earlier irregularities came to an end. But in the main the improvement was in administration rather than in a betterment of industrial or race relations. It is indeed remarkable that even in the large international companies and in the best managed of the large copper mines, the overall functions of personnel management can still not be adequately performed because the quality of many of those selected for the task leaves so much to be desired. A knowledge of African languages and customs is still regarded as an important qualification even though the language spoken might be that of only a fraction of the Africans employed. All too often the appointments are made because the individual has proved unsatisfactory in some other form of employment or has reached retiring age.

The behaviour of many European supervisors, their frequent dishonesty, their bad manners and all too often their inefficiency, all exercise a real effect upon the particularly observant and receptive African. These are the Europeans he knows most about and with whom he comes in closest contact and their behaviour has considerable influence on his attitude to Europeans in general and his attitude to work.

In common with the Union of South Africa, the two Rhodesias have restricted the type of work in which non-white labour can engage so as to give the maximum protection to Europeans on the lower rungs of the industrial ladder. These restrictions differ from those in the Union primarily in that they are not enshrined in the law but rather in the implications of the law. By various devices, such as by limiting the use of the term 'employee' to Europeans only in industrial legislation, Africans have been successfully excluded from undertaking skilled work. In Northern Rhodesia there is less restriction than in Southern Rhodesia but this distinction is only a matter of degree. When, for example, a European wants to build a house in Southern Rhodesia he will, if he wants the bricklaying done cheaply and well, employ an African to do the work. It will cost him five or six times less than if he were to engage a European bricklayer. But the snag comes when he wants other craftsmen, such as plumbers or electricians, skills that the Africans have not yet been trained to perform. It will subsequently prove very difficult, even impossible, to get a European electrician to wire his house if the bricks have been laid by an African. It is therefore possible for Southern Rhodesia to boast that they have no discriminatory industrial legislation. They do not need it as things are, but the effect of current practice upon the African is the same and probably causes more bitterness than if such practices were set out in the law.

Roughly speaking, the African's ceiling is the European's floor. Accordingly, Africans who have received a fair education (and these are increasing yearly) and those who possess some natural ability, find the continued subservience to Europeans with inferior training or mental qualities extremely galling. Such Africans frequently state that they prefer life in the Union of South Africa, where many of them have received their training, although the degree of discrimination may well be the same. These men are not impressed by the frequent utterances of government officials and others to the effect that there is no 'civilized labour policy' in Southern Rhodesia or that the policy of the country gives equal rights to all civilized men. Deep and ugly distinctions exist and are an every-day experience and the fact that these occur beneath a cloak of liberalism is regarded as rank hypocrisy.

The Committee of Enquiry investigating the protection of secondary industries in Southern Rhodesia recommended in 1946 that, '. . . . since any bar to the employment of the urban native in the capacity in which he is most productive is opposed to the interests of both European and native workers, efforts be made to check the colour prejudice in the labour policy of Southern Rhodesia.' Unfortunately, this recommendation has received little support and, though Africans have won some footholds in European-held posts in the past few years, notably as bus drivers and conductors, each success has only been achieved at the cost of increasing European hostility and fear of further encroachment on their chosen preserves.

In western society, social pressure and the desire for wealth are probably the most important incentives prompting men to work. Neither can exercise any great influence over the urban African in existing conditions. In tribal life the slacker or the loafer was seldom tolerated. As a general rule, ridicule and the fear of losing the co-operation of kinsmen were sufficient sanctions to keep men working at their various tasks. In town neither of these sanctions can be effective because the work performed by men has little or no direct bearing on or advantage to his rural relatives. Kinsmen are, therefore, largely uninterested in whether their urban cousins work well or, in fact, whether they work at all. In the towns, moreover, no form of public opinion exists to control group or individual behaviour. It is, indeed, unlikely that public opinion will ever develop while Africans have no right to ownership of land or long-term security and while the status of those who have achieved some education or success continues to receive no official recognition.

Most Europeans make no attempt to conceal their preference for the uneducated African and they do all they can to avoid or even to slight those whose education has lifted them above their fellows. In government circles such a policy is obviously impractical but even so, many civil servants go as far as they can to avoid making any kind of concession to the better-educated African. The Chief Native Commissioner remarked to the writer, for example in 1949, that it was his policy to make no distinction between educated and uneducated Africans. If any of them wanted to sit down in his office they sat on the floor.

Promises of more money for harder or better work have little interest for the urban African because he cannot use the extra money in the way people are accustomed to do in more normally constituted societies. Legislation is one reason for this. The Industrial Conciliation Act, the Land Apportionments Acts and the Urban Areas Act of Southern Rhodesia all combine to make it extremely difficult for the African to compete economically or politically with the Europeans.

In western society men work for money because of the security that it brings or because of the possessions and the prestige that a wealthy man can command. In African society men also sought security and prestige. These were likewise achieved only by hard work although the concept of money did not enter into the situation. While the European achieves his security or prestige with the money that he earns from working, the tribal African obtained them as a direct result of the work he performed. The urban situation, however, demands that the African should work as hard as, or even harder than, he has ever done before but at the same time, neither his work nor the money that he earns can provide him with the security or the prestige that he would like.

The average urban African is unhealthy, badly housed, uneducated, and he lacks any security in town, even if he happens to have been born there. These are his greatest and his constant worries. The fact that he cannot afford a shilling for a drink of beer worries him as little proportionately as it does the average European. Neither money nor the work that he performs can release him from any of his real troubles. He cannot obtain better health, a better education for himself or for his children, or a better or more permanent home in the urban areas however much he may earn or save. These amenities, although provided free or at subsidized rates, are all in short supply and whenever the African requires any of them, whatever his status, his income, or his background, he must take his turn in the queue.

These various factors determine the African's attitude towards savings and money itself. Savings, for example, can be of two kinds. There is short-term saving for some distinct purpose, and there is long-term saving, usually for some less well-defined end, often concerned with old age or for what would be ill-named in many parts of Central Africa, a rainy day. Saving of any kind, however, is saving up for something and the short-term form of saving is very much more common because few Africans have any definite views or ideas relating to the future.

Few of the objects that the African comes to town to acquire can be purchased with the first month's wage, even if he is in a position to use it for other than living expenses. In most cases, therefore, men are obliged to save for a longer period. Sometimes employers keep back a fixed sum each month; sometimes the money is handed over to a trader under a form of hire purchase although the African will not actually be given the object until he has either paid the full amount or almost all the price asked. Frequently the money is handed over to a senior relative, a procedure that strangely enough seems to cause few disputes. It is reported that much money is hidden in the ground and in some cases even in the cemetery particularly by grave-diggers, who have themselves lost most of their fear of the supernatural and who know that thieves will not venture.

Scarcely any long-term saving is found. As has already been suggested, all saving is saving up for something and the African does not look far into the future both because his past training has never taught him to do so and also because under present urban conditions there is virtually no future for which he can plan. 'Men bow down to the sun that shines brightly in the sky rather than to that which has not risen,' is a saying to which the African generally subscribes.

Under present-day conditions, money can do little more than provide the means of acquiring trinkets or consumer goods, the kind of bric-a-brac that a traveller picks up on his travels. The value that an African places upon its possession differs therefore very considerably from that of those who pay him. He neither needs it so much nor requires to save it to the extent that is found in European society.

The African attitude to gratuities after long years of service and the manner in which he frequently changes his job and often thereafter accepts a considerably lower wage well illustrate his attitude. From time to time gratuities of up to a hundred pounds are paid to Africans working on the railways and elsewhere who have completed twenty or more years service. Whenever such gratuities are made the fact is well ventilated by the authorities in the local press. To a European accustomed to African poverty, the award of even fifty pounds may seem as something in the nature of a real windfall. It does not create the same impression on the African. He sees men and women living in nearby government and other compounds granted periodical permission to brew beer and earning just as much in a few hours. There is therefore little inducement to remain in the employ of a single firm for life and forgo perhaps the only freedom that the urban African has of changing his master when he likes, all for a sum of money that he does not especially need and which is easily enough earned by brewing beer over one weekend.

Every employer of African labour will have encountered cases of Africans leaving and subsequently accepting a considerably lower wage in a new job. Domestic servants who leave well-paid and apparently comfortable jobs in European homes will accept industrial employment at a fraction of their previous wage. Many cases are known in which African boss boys will willingly change their job and work in other concerns in which they have no authority at all. Thus, the Rhodesia Railways once instanced a man earning ninety-five shillings a month as a boss boy who went home on leave without permission. He returned to the railways in due course where he quite willingly accepted a job in another section to that in which he had been working at thirty-five shillings a month and with no gratuity rights accruing from his earlier service.

Such practices are not so strange if seen in the light of African traditional behaviour, of their general attitude to money and of the conditions under which they live in the towns. Indeed, instances that are not altogether dissimilar can be found in the British industrial scene as well. The Welsh coalminer who when asked why he turned up to work only three times a week, replied that he did so because he could not earn enough in two days, obviously had an attitude to money similar to that of many Africans. And the attempts made by the National Coal Board to induce miners to work harder by organizing dress shows for their wives is a further illustration.

One African once replied to the question as to why he moved from a higher to a lower-paid job by saying, 'We do not work for money alone.' He went on to explain that he changed his job in order to mix with new faces in a new environment. This is not an uncommon idea amongst the urban Africans and springs from the way of life they lead.

In European civilization we are accustomed to do certain things and to meet certain kinds of people in our teens and as we grow older we meet new kinds of people with new kinds of interests. All the time life is changing for us and though we may not notice this change, our interests are constantly being moulded to a new environment, to a new attitude to life and to new surroundings.

No such development takes place in African urban society automatically. It matters little whether a man is sixteen, twenty-six, thirty-six, forty-six or even fifty-six. He does the same kind of work and is treated in the same way. He is an everlasting 'boy'. He is thought of largely as a child and treated as one by his masters. Football is the only kind of recreation he is considered to need and he receives virtually the same rate of pay and lives with the same kind of people all his life in town. He can never get away from the environment that he entered when he first came to town possibly at the age of eighteen.

It irks many older men to work and live alongside others considerably younger than themselves and less mature. Their intelligence, their interests and their powers of observation are changing constantly and they need intellectual stimulation, even if the level required to satisfy them for the present is lower than a European might demand. At present, the only way they can find the change and stimulation that they desire is to move to a new environment in which their particular interests or age group are better represented. So there are many changes of job and of home. Money being of less importance than life they do not feel the compelling pull of a higher wage offer as do Europeans and when they want to make a change, money is unlikely to dissuade them. Perhaps their education is not as great as ours or perhaps they are really better educated for living. It will no doubt be possible one day to teach—or more likely to force—the African to put cash first in his rating of what matters in life. But a lot of ugly consequences will follow the creation of an urban proletariat of wage slaves. For one thing the African today is not usually desperate when he strikes for more pay. He always has his friends to help him and usually he has a home in the country to which he can go if the worst happens. Consequently he does not have to use desperate methods. When, however, the Africans have nothing to rely on but their wages they will probably work harder, but when they come to strike they will be desperate men and they will use desperate means.

The present situation is no more to the liking of the African than it is to the Europeans although the focus of each race's attention is centred on a somewhat different aspect of the problem. The Europeans for their part are chiefly concerned with the low level of African productivity. The Africans, on the other hand, barely give this matter a thought. The bars to progress are very real to them and they know that, under present conditions, town life in European employment can offer them little in the way of lucrative employment or future stability. Consciously or unconsciously, therefore, they refuse to cut themselves completely adrift from their tribal kinsmen and their tribal background.

This tendency to live and work in town while maintaining unproductive land in the reserves is referred to as the 'foot in both camps' attitude and is largely condemned on the grounds that a man who attempts to retain a foothold in both places cannot be efficient in either. There is considerable truth in this assertion although it is erroneous to speak of men having one foot in the town and one in the country, for no man can be said to have a foot in the town. The actual situation is that the urban Africans are poised between two different ways of life or systems of belief. They see clearly enough that the kinship system of tribal days and the monetary system of the west are incompatible. They see the two systems in conflict and they want to come out on the winning side. At present, however, neither side can offer any long-term advantage. The monetary system of the west offers goods but no security. The kinship system offers few goods but some security. This security, however, is already somewhat suspect because of the break-up of the tribal order. On the other hand, the precarious state of those who are completely detribalized, who have no country home to retire to in their old age, or who have no knowledge of country life, is fully realized. And so the majority of men continue to sit on the fence and attempt to retain such rural security as is available together with as many of the material benefits of town life as they can obtain.

Those Africans who have been born in town or who have cut themselves off from the tribal areas irrevocably, must make the best of what urbanization has to offer. The brightest amongst them are quick to see that for all their criticism of the Africans' 'foot in both camps' attitude, the Europeans themselves are in their own way equally two-footed, for many of them regard Africa as a place from which they propose to extract the maximum amount of money possible before returning 'home', as the majority still call Britain.

So far no specific mention has been made of wages save to indicate that they are generally inadequate. A definition of inadequate would of course depend upon whether one is referring to the needs of the

African or the value of his work. There can be little doubt that the Africans' actual earning capacity is low, and although no such studies have been made, it could probably be shown that his earnings were not low in relation to his output. Such, however, is an academic argument, although business men would seize and use it with enthusiasm if it could be proved. The African has to live and in order to live he has to be able to buy enough food, clothing and amenities to make life reasonably worth living. Herein lies the problem, for the cost of most goods in the Federation are inflated by reason of the high wage structure of the European population. In a country in which train drivers earn well over a hundred pounds a month and in which miners working underground can earn many thousands of pounds a year—during the height of the copper boom towards the end of the 1950's, rock breakers on the copper belt were earning over £900 a month—it is inevitable that the cost of living should rise well above the means of the African section of the population.

In most countries wages are a matter of bargaining in which breaking point comes when the workers have to decide whether to press their demands beyond a line that may drive the less competent concerns out of business or force increasing mechanization on their employers. Such a situation does not occur in Central Africa in so far as the African workers are concerned. Only very recently have African trade unions come into being as an effective force in Northern Rhodesia, while in Southern Rhodesia there are still many obstacles in their path. In both countries—as in Nyasaland—wages tend to have been calculated either by wages boards, commissions of enquiry following African disturbances or, more usually, following the decisions of individual employers to raise wages in line with a cost of living index based upon an imaginary African's minimum needs of health and decency. It goes without saying that this latter approach, by far the most common, is bound to fail. In order to determine a wage that will enable an African to maintain health and decency, if no assessment of individual worth is to be considered, a knowledge of social and economic conditions is required that goes much deeper than a study of the retail cost of basic food and clothing. This purely mechanical assessment of a minimum wages does not recognize human variations or human aspirations in any form. The African, like any other person, is not a machine whose output can be gauged or controlled by the amount of mealie meal, meat, peanuts, salt and other simple commodities which are poured into him each month. He is in every way as human as other people, and he exhibits all the varied urges, needs—imaginary or genuine—and hopes of any other race.

Nor can the African's cost of living, his standard of living or his minimum requirements be measured by European standards or indices. In countries where people are more vocal, and where the planners of budgets and the people for whom they plan are of the same race, every single minimum budget that has been prepared by government or scientific organizations has been bitterly criticized by the people for whom it was supposed to supply the bare essentials of life. This is because even in a relatively homogeneous group, bare essentials to one are luxuries to another.

It is questionable whether it is ever possible to lay down a minimum wage to cover health and decency. For one reason, health is not achieved by food, clothes and accommodation alone. Mental stimuli, desires and urges, all require satisfaction and if they are not in fact satisfied, if the ego is not in good shape, there is a consequent lowering of health. The variety and the nature of the stimuli must vary from individual to individual, based upon the degree of well-being that he has acquired, his frustrations, his family commitments and the means that he has to satisfy these various urges. Thus, there is no justification for postulating any given article at a given price to be essential or for saying that a married man with two children requires this or that, without children so much less, or again that a single man or woman can live on so much. Africans can and indeed do buy secondhand clothing that no European would think of wearing. They keep shoes going long after a European cobbler would refuse to repair them. They mend and improvise to a considerable extent. The monies saved from mending here or improvising there will subsequently be used for the acquisition of other goods considered more essential than new clothes or whole shoes. Each individual is a problem on his own.

The African cost of living is based upon a whole series of unknown or little understood urges and needs. It covers many outlays that do not figure in European society at all, but which are essential to African social well-being. The payments of lobola, fees to native doctors and special costs imposed upon the African in the form of traditional or conventional obligations to relatives are all legitimate items of expenditure that must be taken into account in any assessment of the urban Africans' cost of living. In addition, a close study is necessary of his purchasing habits and of his various other items of expenditure which, though they may appear highly artificial in European eyes, possess great prestige value that cannot easily be ignored by individual men and women.

The urban African can no more withstand the pull of convention or fashion and the urge to follow the European practice than most Europeans can resist doing what their neighbours have done or buying what they have bought. The African buys expensive clothes because to him clothes are the hall-mark of civilization. There is much in European ways that he cannot copy, much that he does not understand. But civilization to the majority means money, education and clothes and of these clothes are the easiest to obtain. They are only easiest, however, in relation to what are believed to be the other bastions of European civilization. They are still expensive. Social compulsion would be regarded as very strong if a European were to spend a month's wages on his wife's dress and the fact that an African frequently does often spend just this on such an item and usually very much more for his own suit, shows how strong such social forces are in urban African society.

It is the same with various items of food. Typical is the growing African demand for white bread. This costs considerably more than a brown loaf of the same size, yet few Africans eat brown bread. White bread is recognized as civilized bread because the Europeans eat it as a rule in preference to brown. The African blindly follows this lead and pays quite a high proportion of his daily wage to do so.

We know in our wisdom that an African need not spend a month's wages on a dress for his wife, possibly six months wages on a suit for himself and that he need not buy white bread, granulated as opposed to brown sugar, fancy crockery or a cowboy hat. Our knowledge of his requirements is, however, based upon our own rather than his environment. These luxuries mean as much to him as nylons or a new hat to the office typist and both will be prepared to go without food, if need be, in order to obtain what they feel they so desperately need. The social factors underlying the Africans' spending cannot be ignored nor can they be greatly changed under present conditions. They are intimately associated with and developed by the way of life the African is obliged to follow. When he earns more wages, when he is better educated and, above all, when he is given the chance to attain some security and prestige in his own community, his spending habits will develop a more normal pattern. But for the moment his present habits are normal to him, and therefore essential features of his cost of living.

In the town itself almost every African is called upon at some time or other to offer hospitality or financial assistance to relations or friends in need. All this hospitality is provided out of wages and in the absence of any scheme for unemployment, relief, sick pay, or old age pensions, it is as well that such a system should still exist. This, too, is a legitimate charge on African wages and one that is never considered in any assessment of his needs.

As a rule the African is obliged to pay more for his food than does the European purchasing the same items. There are a number of reasons for this. Amongst the most important is the fact that Africans purchase in smaller quantities than the statisticians, who calculate cost of living indices, usually imagine. This is because there is a lack of storage space in their homes as well as limited ready cash to buy in larger quantities. There is often, too, a shortage of the basic commodities that an African is believed to live on and when this occurs he has to purchase a more expensive commodity. The cheap cuts of meat are an example. When not available, and a survey by the Federation of African Welfare Societies in Southern Rhodesia once showed that when Africans were paying 1s 3d a pound for meat they were getting 83 per cent bone, the African has either to buy the expensive cuts favoured by the European or go without. Yet another little-known fact is that African storekeepers trading in the African towns frequently charge more for goods than do European traders because of the convenience of shopping near at hand. Then, too, Africans are obliged do all their washing in cold water. This means that clothes have to be scrubbed that much harder with a consequent increase in wear and tear as well as a greater consumption of soap.

All these are factors seldom if ever considered when the African cost of living is computed. They may not necessarily add up to more than a few shillings a week but there are in fact so few shillings available, and so many calls upon them, that every penny counts.

No mention has as yet been made of one very large group of African employees, the domestic servants. These people represent some 30 per cent of the total labour force but they are of far less importance as a group than their numbers might suggest. As a body they are quite distinct from those of their fellows who work in industry, commerce, agriculture or in the mines. Up to a point domestic service is a skilled trade. It demands a certain standard of English, a knowledge of European domestic arrangements often including cooking, and a willingness to work late hours.

Men working in industry enjoy a greater freedom of action than domestic servants but very few of them are as well off materially. Domestic servants' wages, usually paid monthly, vary according to the type of work done, the time the individual has been employed and the skill of the man concerned both in his work and in individual negotiation. Very rarely do they earn less than men in industrial employment and of course they receive accommodation, rations, cast-off clothing and scraps from the table. Unlike industrial or commercial employees, domestic servants can utilize all their wages as pocket money.

Because it is with domestic servants that the majority of Europeans come in closest every-day touch there is a very marked tendency to take this category of men as the yardstick against which African ability and African thought is measured. Such a practice gives a completely wrong conception of African development and of the crucial problems of race relations in the Federation. Domestic servants are in very few ways typical of the urban community. They are frequently to be seen in the African townships and in the beer halls but they are essentially visitors, moving amongst people whose problems, whose way of life and whose thoughts are quite different to their own. They do not belong to the hurly-burly of town life, they experience few of its tensions and they take little part in political organizations.

Perhaps their only significance, although the importance of this cannot be overrated, lies in the fact that they, more than any other section of the African community, see the Europeans off their guard, and a domestic servant can always command an eager audience as he recounts tales of European misdemeanours or of the indiscretions of mistresses. Indeed, the African domestic servant talks about his European masters and mistresses far more often and in a far less flattering manner than they ever talk about him and the tales lose nothing in the telling. In particular, stories of the seduction of African servants by European mistresses are bandied around and, whether true or false, they create the impression that the European is a very much more venal creature than the African.

Europeans face a dichotomy in their approach to the problems of African efficiency. As industrialists they would like to see the obstacles to progress swept away. As citizens, usually spurred on by their wives, they think differently. Most have therefore compromised and they tend to resort to purely mechanical types of incentive and a variety of devices have been introduced to make the African labourer as efficient a producing machine as possible. Tasks have been broken down to the lowest possible denominator, supervision has been intensified, and monetary rewards in the form of bonuses and piecework rates have been tried. Up to a point all these different approaches work, but they are, in the last analysis, only expedients. The African will not further improve his output or his efficiency because, generally speaking, he is either content or apathetic, and he sees no good reason why he should work any harder. The effort required is disproportionate. He has, moreover, learnt to exist on a wage that barely provides the essentials of health and decency by a process of begging from his relatives, sharing with his friends, resorting to certain illegal or immoral forms of earning, and often going without.

Industry has probably done as much as it can, under existing conditions, to increase productivity. No further improvement can be expected without government intervention, for it is largely as a result of government policy, implemented by the municipalities, that the urban African is in his present plight. As a start it will be necessary to determine, after taking all points of view into account, the form that the urban African community should take. There are only two alternatives for this and no compromise is possible. The government can maintain existing legislation and build up a migrant community without any permanent roots in town. Alternatively, plans can be laid for the development of a settled community which has few, if any, links with the reserves or the traditional tribal system.

Each of these alternatives possesses for the Europeans certain advantages and certain disadvantages. The migrant community is not efficient by normal standards, but its low level of productivity is to some extent offset by the fact that such people need fewer costly social services than a settled community. Migrants can be housed in barrack-like rooms and they require only limited schooling and hospital facilities. Perhaps their greatest advantage is that they make few political demands and do not challenge the paramountcy of European interests in the urban areas. If this latter form is chosen then little change can be expected in the low level of efficiency because the motives that are fundamental in prompting a man to work —the desire for security and self-respect—cannot operate. For such people, the shopkeeper and the prostitute must continue to provide the greatest incentives. Upon these two forms of expenditure the migrant squanders his earnings almost to the last penny because he knows, or hopes, that at home in the reserves there is adequate security.

Settled labour is more efficient because, if it really is settled, it has something to work for beyond immediate needs and because the danger of unemployment itself provides an incentive. European employers welcome its greater productivity but they fear the social and political consequences. A settled African community would expect to enjoy the right of self-determination. But this would impinge in many ways on European sovereignty in the towns. It is, therefore, a demand which European municipalities are unwilling to grant.

Politics demand one solution to this problem and economics another. Either solution can be made to work adequately in its own way if implemented with a measure of humanity. The only solution that cannot work under any circumstances is the attempt to combine the less exacting political demands of a migrant with the greater economic advantages of a settled labour force. The present unhappy urban scene is largely the result of attempting such a compromise, and it has been the disadvantages of both systems that have come to the fore. Work and productivity are at the level of a migrant labour force, despite the provision by the European taxpayer of costly social services, such as cottages for married couples and the schools, hospitals and clinics that are required for a community of married people; for, under existing legislation, the people remain migrants at heart and have the migrant's lack of interest in planning for the future. At the same time, the political demands made are of the type associated with a settled community because the majority of the migrants are, in fact, settlers in all senses save in possessing the right to settle.

Many Europeans in the Federation regard the price of obtaining a truly settled African community as too high in political terms. Yet it is not generally realized that the African pays a greater long-term price than does the European if he is to attain full membership of a western society. He gives up the many advantages of the tribal system of social security and enters a highly competitive economic system in which as yet there is no unemployment relief, no old age pension schemes or ancillary benefits, and for which the vast majority of his fellows are unprepared either by education or tradition. He may gain certain political advantages by the change but his economic difficulties will have only begun.

Any discussion of productivity and incentives comes back ultimately, therefore, to issues that are almost entirely political. If for one reason or another European employers of African labour and their Government regard the concessions that would have to be made to attain greater productivity as too great and the political conditions that would result as undesirable, little point is served in maintaining the pretence of developing urban family life. If the African is not to be given security of tenure in the urban areas, or the opportunity of belonging to an established system, then migrant labour, for all its many drawbacks, is likely to be the most effective labour on an overall cost basis in the long run.

On balance it is impossible not to feel a great overwhelming sympathy for African men and women resident in the towns of Central Africa. But it is yet equally possible to sympathize with the Europeans who have upon their very doorsteps this almost monstrous human problem.

CHAPTER 7

Today's Masters

The army saying that there are no bad soldiers but only bad officers can in some senses be applied to Central Africa. The badness of the African rank and file is in many respects regrettably obvious. Most of the fault for this badness must, also regrettably, be laid on the shoulders of the Europeans. Like their fathers before them, the European settlers have failed to win either affection or respect from the African native. And, again like their fathers, the technical achievements that they have created in Africa and much that they have done for the Africans arouses world-wide admiration. The giant copper mines of Northern Rhodesia, lying beyond hundreds of miles of dense scrub, are a remarkable memorial to European industry and perseverance in the face of many hardships and disasters. The whole system of communications through the territory, the roads, bridges and railways have all been developed in the face of difficulties that people who regard the Europeans of Central Africa as pleasure-loving idlers cannot possibly imagine. After long years of struggling against every kind of adversity the mines, factories and commercial enterprizes have begun to show profits. The post-war years have in consequence seen a steep rise in the European standard of living to a level that few other countries can boast. It is true that much of this development has only been possible because of African co-operation, but the inspiration for it, the planning, the financing of it and all the risks that were taken in the process were European and European only. It is these technical achievements and the very nature of the country, its spaciousness and the backwardness of its inhabitants, that have together played a considerable part in creating the character of the European inhabitants and, as they like to call it, the Rhodesian way of life.

Perhaps the most pronounced feature of this Rhodesian way of life, at least to an outsider, is the amount of leisure that all sections of the European population seem to enjoy. This does not mean that they are idle. Rather it is comparative. They probably work as long hours as do people in England. But when they are not working they are not obliged to devote as much time to domestic chores that so many husbands and wives in Europe and America accept as normal. Indeed the Rhodesian situation differs markedly from many other countries, not only in the amount of spare time available for recreation and other non-working pursuits, but also in the fact that husbands and wives can share equally in all the advantages of a high standard of living.

In Britain the increasingly affluent society has tended to benefit husbands rather more than wives, largely as a result of the taxation system. A husband in England, by judicious use of his expense account, can wine and dine his business associates and contacts far better and in considerably finer style than any but a minority can achieve on their own resources at home. There is also the tendency of many industrial organizations to provide their middle and senior executives with various adjuncts to gracious living in the shape of beautiful furnishings in offices, large and expensive cars, and every luxury whenever the individual is called upon to travel. But owing to a tax system that discriminates heavily against increasing incomes, a man can only marginally improve the standard of living of his wife as his own spending opportunities grow each year. Consequently, the benefits of a higher appointment and a wider range of privileges are very much more for him than for her.

In America the situation is again different. As a general rule American husbands work extremely hard and they take home a much higher proportion of their large incomes than do their counterparts in Britain. But they are worried men, troubled alike by the pressure of competition, their ulcers and a high incidence of stress diseases. The American business man is the highest-paid executive in the world but it is in fact his wife who has the real benefit of these earnings and whose standard of living is really high. American wives own, for various reasons peculiar to American history, the bulk of the wealth of the country and they enjoy a much more relaxed and more active leisure than their husbands.

In Central Africa the high standard of living is uniquely enjoyed by husband, wife and children in equal proportion. Indeed the taxation system of the country is such that this high standard of living can be enjoyed by almost all Europeans since a married European has to earn £800 a year before he starts to pay income tax at all.

It is sometimes jokingly remarked that a pedestrian in Rhodesia is a man with only one car. It is, however, true that Southern Rhodesia has more cars proportionate to its white population than any other community in the world apart from California. Another statistic that supports the evidence for a high standard of living is that there are more millionaires in Southern Rhodesia than in Britain. Prosperity in Northern Rhodesia is of more recent growth and derives almost entirely from the expansion of the copper mines in the postwar years and to their present rôle as the largest provider of foreign currency in the Federation. For many years before the war the Northern Rhodesia miners and farmers were very badly off in relation to those in Southern Rhodesia. Since 1946, however, their wealth has increased enormously. Reference has already been made to European rock breakers earning over £900 a month. Although salaries have not advanced so steeply, the copper bonus that is based upon the selling price of the metal has made the Rhodesian copper miners extremely well off.

On the whole the money does not seem to have brought them a lot of joy. Although the mining authorities do all they possibly can to offset the fact that the copper belt is a very long way from anywhere and that the climate is somewhat oppressive, yet each mine is, for all the lavish expenditure on amenities, public gardens and sporting facilities of every kind, still a small enclosed world in which 'shop' is the main topic of conversation. In each of these small worlds there is far more grumbling about the things people have not got— often things that they never could have in the circumstances—than there is contentment at the many things they are given. Typical of this attitude to life and the new-found wealth it has brought to the majority is the story of one European shop steward and a firm supporter of the Mine Workers Union. His particular situation was that he had been working on the mine for about eight years, he and his wife lived rent-free in a company bungalow in the mine township, electricity, water, furniture were all provided free and even electric light bulbs were exchanged by the company when they failed. The man himself owned a large American car while his wife possessed a small British model for her shopping; their two teenage daughters were both at boarding school in Cape Town and every three years the family flew home to England for four months holiday that included a motor trip on the continent. Had this man remained in England he might perhaps have been able to afford a small car, but his daughters would undoubtedly have gone to the local government school and his holidays would hardly have taken him very far or very often from his native Wales. Yet living at a standard which he would never have dreamt possible before arriving in Rhodesia, his main preoccupation in life, judging by his conversation, was to decry management in general and the management of his own particular mine in particular for their exploitation of himself and his fellow workers.

It is difficult to generalize about the social behaviour of the European settlers as a group. No detailed studies have been made, and in any case, people living in the towns lead quite different lives to those working on farms or on the smaller mines. The very nature of the communities differ for obvious reasons. Wherever they live, however, the climate and the plentiful supply of domestic servants makes possible a range of sporting facilities and social life rarely approached today in other lands. Homes with two or three servants are the rule. Many have a great many more and few are without any African domestic help at all.

Men of all ages seem pre-occupied with sport. News broadcasts are heavily loaded with local sporting results, and the wearing of club blazers—largely an adolescent practice in Britain today—is a mark of athletic status still sought after by the middle aged. Women join their menfolk in outdoor games to an extent never known in Britain. Bridge parties are extremely common, often starting early in the morning and continuing throughout the day. Wives, if they have not got a job, have very little to occupy their time other than along the lines already indicated.

Families are not unduly large, indeed four children is quite an exceptional number. In the better-to-do households there is often a European nursemaid. These girls represent the one group of Europeans who are not recognized members of any group and unlike shop girls, typists or receptionists, they are very rarely accepted socially. Most European families can afford African nursemaids who, though not as reliable as male African servants in the home, are nevertheless a useful standby as baby-sitters when the occasion demands. Such occasions do, in fact, demand fairly frequently and sundowner parties, as they are locally called, are very popular.

Drinking throughout the Rhodesias is heavy by any standards. Even in South Africa where the cheapness of local wines, brandy and beers makes for a heavy expenditure on alcohol, the Rhodesians are looked upon as having an unduly pronounced partiality for the bottle.

Sex behaviour is difficult to generalize about. Communities are small and one might expect a somewhat higher standard of morality than is believed to exist in larger contemporary societies in Europe. Cases were certainly noted where promotion on the mines was denied to those who transgressed normally approved standards of morality. But the very nature of the environment is conducive to a certain laxness. Money has usually come quickly, there is uncertainty about the ultimate future and there is the climate that Byron in his *Don Juan* recognized as a potent force of transgression :

'What men call gallantry, the Gods adultery,
Is much more common where the climate's sultry.'

There is also leisure, wealth and often boredom. These forces in combination are too much for many Rhodesians. In the towns and in many of the farming areas the distinctions normally recognized between intra-marital and extra-marital are not too finely drawn by those who are no longer young enough to pass the time in the sporting pursuits of adolescents. Divorce is easy and cheap and the Federation has one of the highest rates in the world. There are tales of car-key parties in which at the end of a party all car keys are placed in a hat and the women go home in the car whose key they draw out.

Much of this may be put down to high spirits and fun and no doubt there is also much of it that is fairly innocent. Indeed the story goes that often when such parties occur a husband, having taken one of the women home and nothing very wicked having taken place, drives back to his own home only to find his own wife still out. Rather than appear to have been less successful he then drives off into the night alone and he circles the district in his car until he feels his wife will be home and he can return in the rôle of Casanova. Whether these husbands meet each other as they drive around is not known.

In many respects the tales told of Happy Valley in Kenya in the 1930's are being repeated in the Rhodesias and it is not surprising that a large number of thoughtful people send their teenage children away whenever they can.

It is not only the high standard of living that shapes the Rhodesian character and establishes the Rhodesian way of life. The spaciousness of the country is an important factor as is the backwardness of the majority of the native inhabitants. Spaciousness leaves its mark on anyone who has lived for any time in Central Africa. Its effects are discernible in various traits of character and it produces a number of odd paradoxes. Rhodesians are of necessity more self reliant than people who live in Europe. There are no plumbers, electricians, fitters and welders just round the corner who are prepared to call round at the ring of a telephone. Rhodesians must work out their own salvation in many fields and the independent attitude that such a situation breeds has as its obverse effect a measure of intolerance. Like the American from the Southern States, the Rhodesian is friendly, generous and always willing to go out of his way to be of assistance. At the same time he is often bigoted and narrow minded. Like the Americans, too, he likes talking about and identifying himself with extravagant and larger-than-life characters. This makes him feel more on terms with the vastness of the country and to have the numerically preponderant black man kept small in psychological stature only increases that feeling.

Almost every town can boast of one or more of the legendary figures whom the Rhodesians so admire. There was Thomas MacDougall who pioneered sugar planting in the Low Veld and who dragged all the equipment he needed for his mill up from South Africa over roads and bridges that barely existed. Then to irrigate his plantation he spent seven years cutting a 1,400-foot canal through solid granite using only pick and shovel. Needless to say, when in 1922 the town of Fort Victoria elected to secede from Southern Rhodesia, Thomas MacDougall was the natural choice for minister of war in the cabinet that was hastily set up. Ndola in Northern Rhodesia had a mayor who was as notorious in his own way as MacDougall. This man used to increase his own standing with the usually thirsty copper belt miners—and no doubt the dignity of his office also—by challenging and defeating an elephant to a beer-drinking match.

People who identify themselves with such larger than life characters are likely to be more gullible than are other people, such as the British, where the 'Little Man' is far more the national ideal. Just how gullible they are was well demonstrated in the way in which most Europeans in the Federation accepted the famous massacre plot of 1959 with all the inconsistencies that were immediately apparent.

Up until the immediate post-war years, the Europeans could have been considered for all intents and purposes as a single class. Some were richer than others, some held high positions in government and industry employing many hundreds of Africans, others ordered none save an occasional African employee. But they were all of one stamp, one viewpoint, narrow in outlook, tough and endowed with much courage. The post-war industrial boom drove a wedge into this once homogeneous group. The richer whites, numbering in their midst many of the new immigrants, have become richer and the poor have become relatively poorer. As this monetary division has occurred, the two groups have also come to think in somewhat different ways. The reason for this divergence is the appearance of the African as a competitor for the rungs at the bottom of the ladder. It is true that the opportunities for such competition are still extremely limited and every obstacle is placed in the way of any further progress. Nonetheless, economic forces have proved stronger than blind prejudice and the Africans are assembling in ever-increasing numbers at the bottom of this ladder, ready and able to slip into the shoes of any unskilled or semi-skilled European just as soon as the opportunity offers or an employer feels it uneconomic to continue paying high wages to Europeans when Africans are able and willing to undertake the same work at a much lower rate.

Such openings are becoming increasingly common and it is on this issue of African advancement that the two classes of Europeans are most divided. Those who are rich and have secure positions, inviolate not only to the African but also to their fellow whites, would like to see more African craftsmen, more African junior managers, more African appointments in civil service and government. The Europeans who now occupy the jobs for which Africans are clamouring are fully aware of the economics of the situation, of the high cost the country pays, not only economically but also in terms of increasing tension, for the maintenance of what in South Africa is called a 'civilized labour policy'. But the country's needs do not carry much weight and African advancement is fought at every point. Most white trade union leaders admit that they cannot win in the long run.

But it is more than their job is worth not to fight for every white privilege just as long as they can.

Divided though the Europeans may be on the question of African advancement, they yet share two traits in common that are fundamental in the present context. They are singularly parochial, a symptom of culture shock already described, and both old-time settlers and newly-arrived immigrants practice the same form of racial exclusiveness. Today this exclusiveness is more usually called the 'colour bar', but by giving such practices the former name it is easier to show the connection between the behaviour of present-day Rhodesians and that of their fathers and grandfathers in other lands.

History records innumerable parallels to the social situation now developing in Central Africa. The game has been played out many times before—in every clime and continent—by every race and beneath the banner of every creed. Invading aliens settling in other peoples' territory—whether sailors, soldiers, adventurers, colonists, seekers after treasure, escapists, fugitives or traders—all encountered the social problems that arise when a known way of life is left behind and one settles down amidst strangers whose language, social customs and beliefs are different.

Settlers, however, do not believe that history has anything to teach them for they do not agree that the situation they are facing in Africa has any similarity with what has gone before or that is occurring elsewhere. Foreign news, other than important sporting events, is covered extremely briefly in the Federal press and even the Accra Conference of 1958, at which so much of the future policy to be followed by African leaders was discussed, received only the barest coverage. The Europeans certainly recognize the growing threat of African nationalism and African competition but they have solved every problem they have met in the past and it would be out of character for them to run for help the moment a new and unexpected danger threatens.

So, these settlers ask only to be left alone to find their own solution to a problem that, quite wrongly, they believe to be unique and for the solution of which they do not propose to draw any lessons from other lands. While it is possible to admire this spirit of self reliance, one's respect is somewhat chastened by the fact that if the settlers fail, it will be necessary for British troops, paid for by the British taxpayer, to restore law and order once blood has been spilt.

When the Rhodesian is rebuked for his exclusiveness for the operation of a colour bar, his reply is almost always of a similar order. 'Would you,' he asks, 'mix socially with your gardener or the man who delivers you groceries?' A reply of this kind makes it quite unworthwhile continuing the discussion. Yet his answer does perhaps illustrate in a very telling way just how ignorant the average settler is of the Africans of whom he speaks so disparagingly. He genuinely thinks that all Africans are of the houseboy, delivery boy type. He neither knows nor cares about the African teachers, priests, business men and those who have worked through a university curriculum. The Land Apportionment Act and public opinion together ensure that the opportunities that Europeans have of ever meeting these advanced Africans are almost non-existent. The two groups live in separate areas, they rarely if ever meet at work and in the great majority of cases they cannot ever meet in church. Public opinion very effectively ensures that liberal-minded people—or cranks, as those who invite Africans to their homes are called—are made to feel socially very ill at ease.

Were the settlers to be consistent in their exclusiveness there would probably be less African resentment than is actually the case. But in a curious way the settlers and their wives permit of a far greater degree of intimacy with African servants than is usual in most countries and they impose on them far fewer forms of segregation than they do on those Africans who are intellectually and often morally their equals. Servants are the only Africans to whom the average male settler will talk in a normal manner. Women settlers, for their part, permit many intimacies strangely inconsistent with their publicly avowed disgust of Africans and all things African. African servants wash and iron every item of their clothing, they make their beds, see them in various stages of undress and, of recent years, are said to be permitted to bathe in the family bathroom. In the light of this behaviour, for African servants are always assured of an attentive audience when they go down to the local beer hall for a drink, the severity with which the educated African is segregated is very greatly resented. Such people do not want to marry into the settler community. They merely want to be treated as normal human beings and have some degree of recognition in relation to the level of their achievements. They would like to mix socially when there is a common purpose and pursue their own ends when the occasion demands. It might be supposed that in the field of sport one might find the greatest degree of innocuous common purpose and therefore some possibility of social mixing. Yet in Southern Rhodesia there is virtually no such mixing at all and even in Northern Rhodesia there is much ambiguity. Here attempts to create multi-racial sports facilities have in fact done almost more harm than good and have often humiliated the Africans more than if no such attempt had been made. Thus, two hockey boards were set up, one of which would permit games with Indians and the other not, while at Kitwe, Africans were admitted to the playing fields but not to changing-rooms or lavatories.

Federation seems almost to have increased the number of cases in which Africans have been subjected to public insult, and almost every year from the inception of Federation there have been glaring examples. In 1954 the Land Apportionment Act was amended to make possible the building of the multi-racial university in Salisbury and to permit professional men to practise in the city irrespective of race. This first onslaught on the bedrock of Southern Rhodesian policy evoked a sharp protest from the European electorate and a 'Segregation Society' was formed to prevent any more nibbling with the constitution in a community that had publicly avowed its support for a policy of racial partnership. Two years later two further examples of the same kind of exclusiveness caught the headlines of the world's press. In that time it took the personal intervention of the Prime Minister, Lord Malvern, to have the son of one of the Pakistan Embassy staff admitted to a European school in Salisbury. A little later Mr Stanlake Samkange, a graduate of Fort Hare College, a freelance journalist and a public relations consultant, was invited to speak to the Salisbury Chamber of Industries and he was obliged to make his way up to the lecture-room by the fire escape as Africans could not travel in the lifts.

Even as late as 1959 no hotel in Southern Rhodesia could accept bookings from Africans without the special dispensation of the Minister of Native Affairs and this was only granted for visiting non-Europeans. Further trouble arose when Mr Jasper Savanhu was appointed secretary to the Ministry of Home Affairs. The Government wanted him to occupy a house near the university in a white suburb. But this was too much for the local residents. And so the first African Minister in the Federal Government had to retire to the somewhat sordid environment of an African township where, to compensate for the slight, the Government built him an £8,000 house. Mr Savanhu was himself a popular figure with both Europeans and Africans and some of the Europeans went so far as to admit that if he himself had sought to live alone in one of the white suburbs there would not have been such adverse comment. But, in the words of the *Rhodesia Herald* for January 6, 1960, 'there was doubt about his family'.

Yet another blow to those who sought to implement the idea of partnership was the case of Dr Bernard Chidzero who, while studying in Canada had married a white girl. He was due to return to the University of Rhodesia to take up an appointment as lecturer. But this appointment was never confirmed and the university authorities admitted that his marriage had been 'a major factor' in the decision. There was little doubt at the time, when the very existence of the university in the middle of Salisbury, was causing so much ill-feeling, that no other decision was possible. It would have been the last straw for European parents who had sent their sons and daughters to the university to have them taught by an African who was married to a white wife.

Exclusiveness of this kind is tragic in a country in which black and white people must meet and come to understand each other if any kind of reasonable future is to be assured for the Europeans. What is perhaps not so much tragic but downright stupid is the kind of exclusiveness that is practised by the politicians. Thus Sir Edgar Whitehead had lived for years in the same city as two leading African politicians, George Nyandoro and Robert Chikerema, without meeting them. In 1959 when asked why this was he gave two reasons. He thought he already knew what they would tell him and he feared that if he did meet them it would give them added prestige amongst their fellows.

Such reasons appeared sound enough to Rhodesians. To Englishmen or to people living outside the territory they are beyond comprehension. As the *Central African Examier* put it in December 1960, 'It is a shocking indictment of partnership as it has been practised up to now that Sir Edgar had to wait until a weekend house party in England before he could be brought to dine, converse and go to church with African Rhodesians in a setting of complete social equality.' In the Federal field much the same situation prevails and Sir Roy Welensky did not meet Dr Banda until the two of them were guests at Chequers in 1960.

These examples of exclusiveness all refer to Africans in responsible positions. These are the cases that make the headlines and that excite visiting journalists into vituperative comment. It is not possible to give examples of the many thousands of minor insults that are daily inflicted upon the African rank and file by ordinary European men and women but nothing perhaps sums up this situation better than the fact that during his tour of Central Africa in 1959, the Archbishop of Canterbury was rebuked by a public official for daring to shake hands with an African.[1]

By some strange irony, the Europeans who deride the African on every possible occasion are yet prepared to give dead Africans the same respect that they accord to their own people. Thus I have seen European men raise their hats as an African funeral passes them in the street, whilst strangest of all was the action of the authorities at the Nkana opencast mine. Here bulldozers were clearing soil away in preparation for opencast mining and I noticed that the earth was being taken away in a great semi-circle leaving a small piece of jungle untouched. It appeared that in this piece of jungle there were several African graves of long standing. In order not to cover them up, the mine authorities were prepared to expend a very large sum of money and utilize expensive equipment for many more days than

[1] Reported in the House of Lords Debate, 29th July, 1959.

would otherwise be necessary in order to take the huge mountains of earth they were moving well away from the little graves.

Even examples such as these cannot really bring home to people far removed from the scene how really disastrous to racial good feeling is the effect of bad manners on a people who are daily growing in strength and in awareness of their power. It is of course true that many Africans are unduly touchy, that they are always looking for insults, that they often see a slight where none is intended. Thus, if a motorist blows his horn at an African in the street, the African's first idea is that the man is tooting at him because he is an African and not because he is a bad pedestrian. But even allowing for this touchiness, there is enough evidence of individual bad manners to parallel the behaviour of Europeans in other lands to which reference has already been made. The Report of the National Convention of Southern Rhodesia published in 1960 stated that many Europeans are quite unnecessarily rude to Africans in all spheres of daily contact, while Philip Mason suggests that the uncertainty about the future, which amongst the more thoughtful people reinforces a liberal attitude, is responsible amongst the less well educated for manners that are often insulting and aggressive.

What then is the nature of these bad manners? A few illustrations may perhaps convey the atmosphere far more effectively than generalizations or quotations from authoritative sources. The sight of an African being knocked down by a car that does not then stop is a common enough event. Even more common is the sight of a European car knocking an African off his bicycle and likewise driving on. Such incidents have more lasting impact on those who watch than upon the unfortunate man on the ground. But it is in the shops that the observer will see the very worst kind of European conduct. It may well be that in such places the African meets a lowly-paid European in somewhat special circumstances. Be that as it may, a quietly-mannered African, perhaps even an ordained priest, will ask politely for a packet of envelopes or some other possible purchase. The girl assistant will take whatever it is the man wants from the counter and deliberately throw it on the floor at the man's feet. On frequent occasions an African will be told to take his hat off before he can be served. It is also a common sight to see Africans being kept waiting while Europeans who entered the shop after them are served. One can even see Africans being kept waiting by European shop assistants who have nobody else to serve at all.

Almost every African who, by reason of his standard of living or for some other reason, has cause to shop in the European areas can give illustration after illustration of such practices. That they are philosophic about them, as they are at least outwardly, does not mean that they do not notice and feel strongly. Politicians often refer to such instances as 'pinpricks' when questions on the treatment of Africans in shops, post offices and railway stations come up in Parliament. But these politicians are singularly unaware of the unhappiness and the bitterness that such slights cause and also of the extent to which individual instances of bad manners are passed around the African population. Indeed it sometimes seems that Europeans just cannot see that behaviour of this kind towards Africans is even antisocial. Thus Mr Williams, an Elected Member of the Northern Rhodesian Assembly went so far in one debate as to say on this issue, 'There is no conscious or deliberate colour bar system in the country'.[1] He went on to suggest that the treatment about which Africans complained in shops and similar places was due to lack of facilities. But the last word on this question of bad manners can be left to an African lawyer, Mr Herbert Chitepo. 'Let it not be said,' he remarked, 'that partnership failed, not in Parliament or in industrial relations; but in the shops, on the staricases and at office counters where someone denied to the African his essential dignity as a person and violated his sense of justice and self respect.'

Closely related to the subject of good manners is the question of example. Here the Europeans in Central Africa are on trial twenty-four hours a day. Africans see Europeans not as they see themselves, not as they appear at work, but largely from the viewpoint of house-boys, cooks, valets, garden boys, or chauffeurs. Some years ago I was working on a social survey of an African township and I spent some time in the beer hall listening to the conversation. I soon came to realize that all the vices for which Europeans so often denounce the African were pretty exactly reproduced in the tales about the white master or mistress. The tales lost nothing in the telling. But there was enough truth in these stories to make me realize that the more we preach, the more do we brand ourselves as hypocrites.

It is a matter of comment by many Africans that though people in England are known or believed to treat Africans with very much more respect than is found in Central Africa, those who have just arrived from England soon fall into the established ways of behaving. 'They change their views on the boat' is a remark made both by Africans and older settlers. Yet the reason for this change is not far to seek. All Africans are not saints. They have long learnt to react to the hostility and prejudice of the established settlers. They are, therefore, not the kind of people the average immigrant has been brought up to expect. He often already has a stereotype African in his mind when he arrives, the kind of man painted in the more liberal novels of the Deep South. And no doubt the amiable coon of the music halls has made a contribution to the same stereotype. Be that as it may, the houseboy, cook, labourer of field or factory are not of

[1] Northern Rhodesian Hansard, 6th May 1946. Col. 41.

this stamp in Central Africa. And disillusion soon sets in together with the frustration of having to deal with people whose reactions to normal situations are not of the approved form.

A factor that is of very real importance in the whole complex situation and in the Europeans' attitude to it is the Europeans' almost complete lack of any knowledge about the African. This is commented upon again and again by all observers. Typical is a comment by Clegg that 'knowledge of his (African) ways of living, whether in the town or in the African rural areas, is scanty to the point of ignorance.'[1] Other writers have said much the same, one of the most telling being the remark made by Mr McNamee in his report on African administration in Bulawayo. Commenting upon the fact that the Town Clerk was responsible for native administration in the city, he records '. . . with all due respect to the Town Clerk, I submit that his knowledge of the personal side of native administration amounts to just about nothing. He is inexperienced and probably has never come in contact with the native section of the community as a group.' This lack of knowledge by those in authority over the Africans was brought home to me even more forcibly when, during the course of some research into urban African problems in Bulawayo, I was asked by the Civil Commissioner if I would take him round the native location. This man was responsible for the organization of the local magistrates court and it was his ultimate responsibility that the imposition of the law should be fair. Yet he had held his appointment for a number of years without ever having seen for himself the conditions in which the local Africans were living.

Most of the blame for this lack of knowledge must lie with the policy of exclusiveness. Yet the Federation is full of decent Europeans, living secure lives in the belief that they know the African because they think they 'know' the man in the little hut at the end of the garden, the man who cooks their meals, makes their beds, runs errands for them or brings in the office tea. This knowledge is as a rule demonstrated by a wealth of amusing anecdotes in most of which the African—the native as he is called—is held up to ridicule in one way or another. To most Rhodesians, the only good African is the old-fashioned tribal African. 'You could not find a better man than my old herdsman—or cook—or messenger. I can't stand the educated native.' So it goes on, and of course the educated native cannot stand the European either. But the visitor must learn not to express an opinion if he would learn more. Even asking questions is regarded with some suspicion.

Normally it would be true that the local people would know very much more of the social problems around them than any visitor of a few weeks or months standing. Such is not the case in Rhodesia for

[1] Edward Clegg, *Race and Politics*. Oxford University Press, 1960.

Today's Masters

under existing conditions it is difficult to see how the local European settler can ever hope to know anything about the African that is worth knowing. He never meets the educated African, since such men are either in exile, in jail or if they do have dealings together, then the Africans are far too suspicious to speak openly. Educated Africans are excluded from the Southern Rhodesian Parliament, from most civic organizations or special occasions, from white homes, excluded from all but a few hotels. The European does not know these men even in terms of what they stand for and demand. He does not hear or read their speeches—save perhaps a headline taken out of context by his rather narrow press. He does not converse with them even privately. He cannot therefore know how they have striven to reach their present way of life, the obstacles and the frustrations they have met and overcome, the many problems they still face. Europeans have no idea how Africans feel about being treated uncouthly because they do not believe that they are so treated. They have no idea how Africans feel about being discriminated against by a people they could once have respected and now only seek to copy.

It is an absolute and unassailable fact that the well-read visitor to the Rhodesias or any interested party in London, can know more about the educated Africans than almost any white European settler. And, in the immediate term, it is these educated Africans who are the only Africans that matter.

It might be expected that at least the Native Affairs Department would understand the African problem and provide useful background information about it. It is upon this fiction that the Government relies for such background knowledge as is required to frame legislation. 'The Native Department knows best' has for long been the attitude of successive governments in Southern Rhodesia and to a rather less extent, perhaps, in the two northern territories where there is very much less African urbanization, and what there is, has become increasingly the sole concern of the large mining companies.

The poor quality of the Native Department in Southern Rhodesia derives largely from its history. In the earliest days it had always been hoped that local people would fill appointments in the civil service. Consequently, the Government was under continuous pressure to appoint Rhodesians to junior appointments and this in practice meant boys straight from school. Here then arose an immediate problem. A boy straight from school cannot be given the same responsibilities as one who has gone on to a university and who enters the service some three or even four years later on. The boy straight from school, on the other hand, has to be trained on the job and this is something which few government departments even in Britain are fully equipped to perform. Consequently, these boys were given what Lord Wellesley a hundred years before had called 'the menial, laborious, unwholesome, and unprofitable duty of mere copying clerks'. Typical of this approach was the case of one member of the Native Department whom I met in the Bulawayo office. This man was writing in a huge ledger-type book reminiscent of the kind clerks had used in the eighteenth century. I asked him what he was doing and he replied that he was recording and checking up payment of native dog tax. It seemed a very elementary thing for a man of some thirty years of age to be doing and so I enquired why such work could not be done by an African. The man was uncertain for a moment. 'I don't know, really,' he replied, 'I suppose they could. But I don't know very much about the African.'

This man had completed almost ten years in the Native Department and he was not untypical. The training he was receiving, long drawn out as it was, would make him progressively less fitted to take the broad view. With men trained in this manner the government must of necessity become less and less willing to trust, consult them or they for their part to trust or consult either their subordinates or their native chiefs. As Philip Mason points out, 'This was the danger. Of course there were men who triumphed over the system and there were always men who came in from other walks of life or from the universities; but broadly it was true that men were taken younger than in the Colonial Service and that it took them much longer to reach a position of responsibility. Nor was the official body on the Native Commissioner's side so wholeheartedly as would have been the case in a Crown Colony. In such a colony, there would be as a rule one body of officials, a graduated hierarchy, in which those at the top had in their time served as district officers and district commissioners and still used their basic assumptions. But this was not so here, where "Native Affairs" was not the groundwork of all administration but a separate mystique. The highest to which its practitioners could aspire was not Chief Secretary or Governor but Chief Native Commissioner. And the Chief Native Commissioner, who had not yet become also the Secretary for Native Affairs, was one departmental head among others, liable to be asked questions, through the Secretary, by his superior the Administrator or by the watch-dog of the Colonial Office, the Resident Commissioner; this position did not encourage the confidence that enables a central authority to devolve power. Thus headquarters dared not devolve power to the district and as less and less was left to the Native Commissioner he clung more closely to all he had and devolved less to the chiefs; the whole spirit of the administration turned further and further from the idea of ruling through the chiefs, more and more to a system of strict and direct control.

'Thus instead of being the father of his people throughout the district, the Native Commissioner became the warden of a reserve—a national park where those curious creatures, the natives, could live their lives undisturbed. He and his charges together were an aspect of Rhodesia in which the average Rhodesian elector was not much interested except as a source of labour; "the country is run on the pretence that the native is not here," a Native Commissioner said to me with a certain bitterness even as late as 1956. And more and more it became an unconscious assumption that the reserves were the place where the natives should be; their irruption into the world of cities was something to be covered up decently.'[1]

All this is not to say that in the Native Affairs Department of the Southern Rhodesian Government there were not a number of able and dedicated men. But the system was not such as to encourage them and indeed those who took an interest in the detribalized Africans and gave them a measure of sympathy were unlikely to get very much promotion. The case of B. B. Fitzpatrick is a case in point. Various writers on the Southern Rhodesian scene have commented on this man's almost unique interest in and respect for the Africans —a respect that is also almost uniquely reciprocated—but the authorities have not shown the same recognition of his talents. Typical of his attitude but also not that of his department, was his practice of putting on a dinner jacket when he went down to represent the Government at evening ceremonies organized in African townships. His immediate superior would never have dreamt of paying the local Africans such a compliment, even if he could be persuaded to go down to the African area at all after his office had closed for the day. This latter form of behaviour is typical of the department's attitude to the African, an attitude that makes the sight of any Native Affairs Department official shaking hands with an African one that few people can ever have seen. Even after the Southern Rhodesia emergency in 1960, when Africans were shot in the locations of Bulawayo and Salisbury and when large numbers of Africans were rounded up and locked away, Southern Rhodesian M.P.s still clung to the belief that they needed no direct contact with African opinion. 'The Native Department was most excellent indeed in keeping the Government and the people of the Colony in touch with and controlling the African' was part of a speech made by Mr Went, a government supporter at the time.

All in all, it is hardly surprising that in 1961 the Native Affairs Department, the source of the Government's information about the African and the custodian of his welfare and development, should have been condemned by the Social and Industrial Council of the Diocese of Mashonaland in a reasoned and devastating case in which the Council called for the department's abolition on the grounds

[1] *Op. sit.* pp.279-280.

that its functions bred hostility and its existence perpetuated racial discrimination.

Had the Northern Rhodesia mining companies been better served in their personnel departments, it is probable that they would have been in advance of any other industrial or municipal community in their handling of African affairs. Unlike so many other employers, they have stated clearly for many years their intention to advance Africans progressively. But the trades unions on the one hand and the poor quality of their personnel departments on the other have together contrived to reduce their liberal aspirations to little more than a pretence. Unlike the municipalities, too, they have given access to anthropological and other research workers with the idea of discovering something of the problems facing the detribalized African, the kind of information that no government statistical survey can provide. Unhappily the companies have not been well served in this respect either. The enquiries of some of the anthropologists were suspect on political grounds while others were far too concerned with the African of yesterday and his fast vanishing customs than with the urgent problems of the present.

Ignorance of the true position does not, however, result in the average European settler failing to sense the danger of the situation. His overall approach is to try and main the *status quo* in the illogical belief that any step up for the African is automatically a step down for himself. Yet, even if one condemns such an approach it is still possible to understand the motives that prompt it. Those who criticize must be sure that they themselves and all whom they represent would willingly abandon a position in which the possession of a white skin is an automatic passport to an aristocracy, irrespective of the worth of the individual concerned. In the highly competitive economy of the western world with all its insecurity, it must be very comforting to know that there is always somebody beneath one, that it is not possible to sink to the bottom.

To maintain their present position of dominance, therefore, and to fight every step up that the African attempts, the Rhodesian settlers have developed what appears to the Africans at any rate to be a technique for hiding their real intentions in a series of high sounding principles that derive from the very best traditions of reforming liberals. There is frequent reference in Parliament and in the press to the ideals of partnership, Cecil Rhodes's dictum of equal rights for all civilized men is brought out of the cupboard on every possible occasion; then there is 'the preservation of cultural standards of behaviour' and 'the essential respect for law and order'. It is ironic and also unique that in Rhodesia the African Nationalist leaders are denied the use of the slogans usually employed in such situations because the European settlers have taken and used them already.

Unhappily, the great gulf that exists between principles and practices has long evoked a bitter cynicism from Africans whenever these phrases are uttered. They see only lip service paid to the concept of partnership and they remember Lord Malvern's definition—a definition that was unlikely to have been intended for general use—that partnership in Africa implied the relationship of a man and his horse with the Africans playing the rôle of the horse. For those Africans who wanted concrete examples of European intentions, a study of government expenditure told them all they needed to know. Thus, in Northern Rhodesia, the expenditure on the police force was roughly the same as on education—about a half million in 1951 rising to £2¼ mn. in 1959/60; while in Southern Rhodesia the Government spent twenty times as much on the education of a white boy as they did on a black.

Until the emergency in 1960 the general policy of the Southern Rhodesian Government had been to rely on restrictive legislation and a strong police force. A last attempt at strong-handed methods was tried with the Preventive Detention Bill of 1960 that even the usually pro-settler *Daily Telegraph* was forced to admit was reminiscent of Star Chamber Legislative days. Circumstances, however, proved these methods largely ineffective. Ways and means were found of circumventing most of the legislation while world opinion had become too concerned with events in Central Africa for the use of force—other than an occasional procession of armoured cars through the African townships—to be of any practical use. The settlers therefore brought out their final weapons, delaying tactics, juggling with the constitution, trickery and attempts to divorce the African masses from their chosen leaders.

In their delaying tactics the settlers are fortunate in that they have powerful vested interests at work in the European trade unions. Just as the T.U.C. in Britain can deny responsibility for the irresponsible behaviour of its member unions and thus tacitly condone acts that it must publicly condemn, so in Rhodesia the Government profess themselves unable to interfere in the policies and practices of the large and powerful white unions. This, as it happens, suits the electorate very well. Unable to block outright legislation for African advancement that has already been passed, the European railway workers and the European copper miners have shown themselves nevertheless as adept even as the House of Lords in their capacity for delaying the implementation of legislation. It took, for example, seven years for the mining companies to implement an African advancement scheme on the copper belt, while on the railways the white unions were still in 1961 resisting the advancement of an African to the job of fireman, even after seven years of Government ownership.

Democratic procedures, and especially the franchise, offer almost unlimited opportunity for the settler governments to resort to what in the present context can only be called trickery. All in positions of authority, from Lord Malvern and Mr Garfield Todd onwards, have tried their hand at sorting people out into different voting categories so as to ensure that only those which each considered to be reasonable and responsible men would come to power.

Some of these attempts have honestly tried to ensure a government that would progressively represent all shades of intellect and culture in the community. Others have proved disappointing to the African even to the point of dishonesty.

Almost all the franchise proposals have assumed that the day could come when Africans could be expected to vote along party and not racial lines. Sir Godfrey Huggins took this view in his proposals; Lord Home expressed very much the same hope in 1959. 'The point I want to make was that as more and more Africans qualify for the franchise, the time will come when the African minority will be a majority on the voters' roll, though, of course, when that time comes they should be voting entirely on party lines.'[1]

To imagine such a situation could emerge in Central Africa, or in Southern Rhodesia more specifically, is naïve in the extreme. In Southern Rhodesia, for example, where Africans outnumber Europeans by 13 to 1, there have been 60 years in which the 13 have earned ten times less than the 1, when the 1 has been privileged in all things and the 13 in none. All that has occurred because while the 1 has been in power they have voted along racial lines and used political measures to maintain their position. Given such an example, anyone in authority who can imagine the African will not act in very much the same manner when their turn comes is guilty of a serious lack of judgement.

None of the schemes proposed for increasing African representation were democratic in the sense of 'one man one vote'. But as this and this alone is what the African leaders want, none have ever gained much popular support from the Africans even though as the schemes themselves became increasingly liberal the opposition from European electors increased proportionately. Most of the proposals put forward have been more effective in gaining time for the Europeans and keeping Africans out of government than they have been in achieving the civilized standards of behaviour and culture that they sought to inculcate in those elected to govern.

As each new scheme was propounded, Africans became increasingly sceptical of their worth—and indeed they had every justification for feeling as they did. The first franchise proposals in Northern Rhodesia

[1] Quoted in Press Communique No. 392 Inf. Dept. N.R. Gov. 18th August 1959.

effectively disenfranchised the African population for the foreseeable future by limiting the vote to British subjects of 21 and over. The Africans, apart from a mere handful, were protected persons and not British subjects. They were therefore excluded by virtue of the territory's protective status. A later scheme for Northern Rhodesia and Nyasaland ruled that past and present members of provincial councils should replace representatives from the African Representative Council in Northern Rhodesia and the African Protectorate Council in Nyasaland. Officially this move was to increase the size of the electoral college. In reality and as the Africans were quick to see, it was a means of blocking the more progressive Africans from exercising political control by weighing the electoral colleges with the votes of the older and more conservative Africans who were concerned more with tribal than with urban affairs. Very much the same sort of tactic was adopted in Southern Rhodesia. An enlargment of the Southern Rhodesian Assembly was proposed in 1960 in which the number of seats were increased from forty to fifty. This move was hailed by press and radio as a concession that would enable Africans to become M.P.s for the first time. But with the publication of the Redelineation Commission's proposals, it became clear that there could not be a single African in the new house.

Trickery is not the only ruse to which the settler Governments have resorted in their delaying tactics. There are cases of sheer dishonesty. Thus a firm of public relations consultants operating on behalf of the Federal Government and bent upon giving to the Federal Government a counter to the much adverse critcism they were receiving wrote in a brochure entitled 'Inside the new Africa', that 'A mistaken assumption of most people in Britain is that the overwhelming majority of Africans in the two northern territories is implacably opposed to federation.'

For a government to authorize the publication of a statement of this kind is beyond comprehension. Every visitor to the Federation knows from personal observation how untrue it is. Indeed, the best-known quotation from the very authoritative Monckton Commission report, published only a few months earlier, had stated the complete opposite. 'The dislike of federation among Africans in the two northern territories is widespread, sincere and of long standing. It is almost pathological.'

The final weapon in the European settler armoury is one that has been tried again and again in British imperial history. This is the attempt to discredit the leadership of the emerging nationalist groups. The Rhodesian approach is twofold. In the first place there is an attempt to build up the power of the old and conservative chiefs. The second method is to attempt to drive a wedge between the leaders and the led.

Boosting the illiterate chiefs is an old colonial custom that has achieved a measure of short-lived success in various parts of British Africa. In Southern Rhodesia the power of the chiefs had all but vanished, when, in 1961, the value of these people was suddenly realized. It was felt that they could be used to discredit the young nationalist leaders of the towns and also to put across certain unpopular measures. A conference of chiefs was accordingly called—an unheard of recognition of their status—and, provided they were prepared to accept government policy in regard to land allocation, destocking and other measures, they were courted as never before. Whether the ruse will succeed is highly unlikely. As the *Central African Examiner* pointed out in June, 1961 :

'For the Government to try and place its crown of rural thorns on their heads (they are unsuspicious enough to wear it) is to put them in a position where they will be diametrically opposed to their followers. Needless to say their own influence will suffer in the same way as in the Union of South Africa, where chiefs have to be heavily guarded in areas where they used to be respected and beloved by their people.'

The attempt to discredit local leaders has also been tried with singularly little success in many other places. It is not long ago that Archbishop Makarios was branded a murderer of British troops with whom no British government would negotiate. The same sort of attitude was found in India and Burma. Kenyatta was yet another case of a leader with whom no responsible government could deal. In Northern Rhodesia successive governors refused to see leaders of the African National Congress. Typical of this attitude were the remarks made by Sir Arthur Benson when opening an African Representative Council Meeting in 1958. 'The economic future of the African people of Northern Rhodesia lies in the hands of the African people. The Government has played and is continuing to play its part,' he said. 'It has put the fruit on the tree. But this Government is not going to pick the fruit and put it into the mouths of those who are too lazy to pick it for themselves. I believe that if the Government tried to do that it would have a very difficult job because so many of the so-called leaders of the African people seem to me to spend so much of their energy in talking. A tremendous number of those Africans who are not talking are listening to those who are, instead of getting on with their jobs and making themselves prosperous and helping to advance themselves and the rest of the African people up to European economic standards.'

A statement of this kind is of course half true, and herein lies the danger. It may make little or no impact in Africa where so many non-Europeans, like Dr Moussadeq in Persia and others, have put economic prosperity low in their list of priorities. But coming from so senior an official, many Europeans who think Africans should put their own prosperity before local politics find additional reasons for their condemnation of African leaders. The Federal Government adopted a similar approach to Dr Banda, and in Southern Rhodesia the African leaders have been likewise ignored and condemned. Thus, on August 24, 1954—in the first year of Federation—the President and Secretary of the Northern Rhodesian National Congress were sent back from Southern Rhodesia and described as undesirable aliens and even as late as 1961, Mr Kaunda, the African leader in Northern Rhodesia, had difficulty, on his return from seeing the Colonial Secretary in London, with the Southern Rhodesian authorities when passing through Salisbury and he too was classified as an undesirable alien. Typical of the Southern Rhodesian attitude to African leaders, who from Burombo down to Nkomo have been successively personally ignored though publicly vilified, was the remark of the Deputy Prime Minister at Umtali in 1960 that 'All the so-called nationalist leaders are would-be dictators, with fascist methods and objectives.'[1]

Many senior Government officials use this term 'so-called' in speaking of African leaders as though to imply that nobody but a few extremists recognize their leadership. The remark may well please the European but it is an expensive form of enjoyment for one day these so-called leaders must come to call the tune.

There may well be some truth in some of the criticism that European politicians make of African leaders even though it avails them very little to speak as they do. Revolutions will inevitably throw up scoundrels on the make alongside men of high ideals. Some African leaders are certainly power seekers, immoral, untrustworthy, just as are the leaders of any other community. But the grievances that they voice are genuine and persistent. It is certainly true also that few of the African leaders are representative—in the true sense of the term—of the masses for whom they speak. But it is for this very reason that they speak so passionately. For their desire is that there should be more Africans like themselves, Africans who can read and write, who earn something approaching a decent living, who are recognized by Europeans, even if the Europeans who recognize and respect them, do not live in the same country as they do.

It is true that the majority of African leaders are better off, better educated, more comfortable in their domestic lives than are the vast majority of their followers. But this does not of necessity make them unsuitable leaders from the African point of view, even though such a state may seem unusual in European eyes. That the majority of

[1] At a St Andrews night supper in Umtali on 3rd December 1960.

Africans do not know what federation is and do not really care about it anyway is no argument for ignoring African leaders' objections to it. Once the masses are better informed, better educated and when they have come in closer contact with the Europeans, they too will feel and think as their leaders feel and think now. And in the last resort they will side with those leaders whether they know what they are talking about or not because the leaders are Africans and the opposition is European. That, for the vast majority of Africans—or indeed of any people in a comparable situation—is enough.

Nationalism grows fast in Africa today and over the next decade there will be few Africans who, faced with the choice of siding with African leaders or European colonial governors, will choose the latter. Intimidation may exist to a limited extent But it is kinship, basic preference and long-term interest that prompts all Africans, irrespective of tribe, financial standing, position or faith, to back African leadership rather than white. Many Europeans, and in particular it would seem those in high authority, are misled by the apparent acceptance by Africans of so much discrimination, and the occasional eruptions appear all the more unexpected. Yet the bitterness that exists just below the surface, that the African so often hides with an apparent philosophic smile, is real and burning. 'The truth is,' as Mason puts it, 'that white men have no monopoly of wearing two faces without conscious insincerity. If the European farmer genuinely believes in such abstract ideals as fair play, justice, the equality of all before the law and before God, yet in practice will sometimes behave as though his African dairyman was a being to whom such concepts do not apply, the dairyman too may appear contented and today may say with truth that he takes no interest in politics, yet tomorrow will vote if he gets the chance for the most extreme nationalist he can find—and with no more hesitation than his grandfather displayed when he followed the Mlimo.'[12]

Another European tactic is to condemn the African leaders of trades unions or political parties for their intemperance, womanizing or misuse of party or union funds. Here is a revival of the old exclusiveness based upon the moral standards of the Victorian era, an era when most people in authority or in positions of power subscribed to certain standards of etiquette and social behaviour that have largely vanished today.

It is certainly true that a great many African leaders do not have most of what are called the public school virtues. But criticism of these failings is not taken very seriously either by the leaders themselves or indeed by the rank and file. Africans of all classes, income

---

[1] The African god who is believed to have told the Matabele to rebel against the pioneers and that he would turn the white man's bullets into water.

[2] *Op sit* pp. 328.

groups, religions or countries of origin, know enough of European behaviour in Central Africa today to realize how hypocritical are the people who make such judgements. They know all about the nocturnal prowls of European men seeking out comely young African women on the outskirts of the townships and they know too of the seduction of male African servants by European wives who cry rape only when they are discovered. As to money, Africans know that in European society there has grown up a whole army of accountants, of auditors to check the accountants, because these checks and counter-checks are essential if money is not to find its way into the wrong pockets. Most Africans indeed have a clear grasp of the simple truth that Europeans are not worse than Africans, but collectively and basically not that very much better. Only those Europeans whose conscience is quite clear are really, therefore, in an inviolable position to criticize African leaders. And there are few if any who pass this test.

The European settlers do not see that little will be served if the existing leaders are successfully discredited. If Dr Banda, Nkomo and Kaunda are unsuccessful in winning concessions, those who replace them will be infinitely more hostile and extremist. Guy Clutton-Brock made this point at a Salisbury National Affairs lunch-time address in 1960, 'Perhaps the greatest danger to the peace in Central Africa is the attempt to discredit African leaders which has gone on over the past few years.'

Any account of the European inhabitants of the Federation must deal in the main with evidence that is for the most part unfavourable. This is in line with the situation as it exists. There is plenty of trouble brewing in Central Africa and this trouble derives from the European traditional failure to master the problem of human relations in a fast developing country. Their good points are almost entirely to be found in the technical field and this book does not attempt to survey this particular aspect other than to maintain in passing that some of these achievements have been considerable. There are, of course, liberal people and organizations that in one way or another try to improve the lot of the African. But such a task is not easy. 'To preach liberalism is to invite defeat' wrote the Bulawayo correspondent of *The Times*[1] and indeed liberalism can do more than invite political defeat. It can mean a severe degree of social ostracism.

It might be expected that the Church would be the obvious rallying ground of those who seek reform. Such, however, has not proved the case. There is no doubt that the missionaries could do a great deal more than is at present being done in the urban areas. They are seldom seen at official functions run by their African parishioners and they take little part in local affairs. At African sports meetings,

[1] 11th November, 1958.

school entertainments, social functions, exhibitions of African dancing or even when competitions are organized between various missions, European missionaries are frequently absent.

The missionaries themselves see the drawbacks to the present system clearly enough. The work they are now called upon to do is far removed from anything for which they were trained or that they originally hoped to accomplish. The ever-increasing government attention to medical and first aid work and the welfare work done by Native Department officials and certain special organizations has taken over much of the important but non-secular work that they once did. With the inspection of schools, and all that it entails, goes the continual worry and responsibility caused by the enforced employment of inefficient and often untrustworthy African school teachers who have to be left to their own devices for long periods each year. One European missionary superintendent put it succinctly when he said, 'We are now merely office boys'.

Missionaries in charge of the various denominations in urban areas are accordingly little-known figures who are generally seen only by their adherents when they are in search of funds. Money to pay teachers' salaries is received from the Government, but money for the actual running of the schools, paying priests' salaries and maintaining church and school buildings must be raised from the African community. This is not as easily done as in the old days when a missionary settled down, usually in one place, and made his home amongst the local Africans. He knew them individually and in almost every case he lived nearly as frugally as they. Consequently, when he asked for funds the Africans gave willingly because there could be no question of his needing the money himself to maintain a higher standard of life. The modern missionary can no longer lead the old kind of life for the reasons that have been shown. He takes away their money and they see little to show for it. What they do see is the comparative comfort in which the missionary lives. As so little is known about him, few of his congregation realize that he is ill-paid by European standards or that the car he drives or the fine home in which he lives in the European area do not belong to him. It may be mechanically wise, as the Seventh Day Adventists point out, to exchange their large American cars each year and obtain the latest models. But such arguments are not understood by the Africans. The limit of their understanding is set by their eyes.

Under such conditions missionary work tends to create a feeling of dislike and hostility on both sides. Few European missionaries have a good word to say for their Christian adherents while these latter almost all complain of their missionaries and in particular of the manner in which colour bar practices prevail within the Church itself. African priests and ministers are particularly vocal upon this point. 'European missionaries are good for a few years and then they become like the other Europeans,' is a remark that is frequently repeated. In addition, a number of allegations are made of the manner in which colour bar practices occur in day-to-day contacts with their superintendents. It is claimed, for example, that when an African clergyman accompanies a European missionary on a tour, the European does not treat the African as a colleague. Social differences are maintained throughout the journey. The European makes no provision for food or bedding for the African priests. When they stop for food each boils his own tea and they even eat separately. African ministers also maintain that when they want to see the European superintendent in his home in town, they must go round to the back of the house and wait until they are invited into the kitchen. They state their business in the kitchen and are then told to go. European missionaries are also said to be unwilling to acknowledge either ordained African clergy or their parishioners when they meet in the European areas of the town.

When these allegations were checked through European sources they were found to be true of the many missionaries working in urban areas. So bad was this practice in one particular denomination that an appeal was sent direct to England by the African members for an immediate replacement for the existing superintendent, together with a statement that no European of South African or Southern Rhodesian origin would be acceptable.

These are perhaps extreme cases and it would be wrong to condemn the whole of the Christian missionary effort on their account even though most Africans can quote other similar examples. Wonderful work is done by individuals working in all the denominations but the average African knows little of such cases and the urban African knows even less.

Of recent years the Christian Church has begun to play a more active part in Rhodesian affairs. Indeed they have at last come to realize that they cannot any longer remain aloof from the political arena. All African affairs are political and there are right politics and wrong politics and on balance too much of the latter. In 1959 the Roman Catholic Bishop of Umtali condemned the Southern Rhodesian school system in the words, 'A more thoroughly unjust state of affairs it would be hard to imagine'. This was followed up in 1961 with an even more outspoken attack on the whole system and published by the joint Roman Catholic Bishops of Southern Rhodesia in their pastoral instructions. In this they denounced racialism, saying that 'though many fail to see it, or refuse through sheer selfishness to acknowledge it, the doctrine of racial superiority as taught and practised by many in this country differs little in essence from that of the Nazis'. They gave credit to the Government for attempts at economic improvement, but pointed to the still very real inadequacies of wages, housing that is often unworthy of human beings, the destruction of African family life through the imposed conditions of employment, segregation in education and social life, and the obvious disparity in the quality of land occupied by the country's two major racial groups.

A certain amount of useful work is performed by European welfare societies, women's organizations, industrial and university clubs. But the measure of their effectiveness can be gauged from the fact that they very rarely include any African members. The work done is largely of the charitable kind, done 'for' the African and not 'with' him. It is charity wrapped rather thinly and as charity it does not win much approval from those it attempts to help. A strange thing and yet one that perhaps could be expected is that one encounters more hostility between the various welfare organizations than one does between the black and white races themselves. Africans see these organizations as primarily concerned with making existing conditions more palatable rather than fighting for a new régime. And as they are not prepared to put up with existing conditions for very much longer, they do not support people or organizations, however well intentioned, whose aim is to alleviate the situation. Africans do not want their lot alleviated. They want it changed irrevocably.

Even making every sort of allowance, it is still not possible to paint a particularly attractive picture of the European master in Central Africa. But it has not been an unfair picture, for a situation so full of bitterness and resentment—as is clear from even a cursory reading of the daily press—could not derive from the actions of people basically fair and well intentioned. After the Nyasaland disturbances fo 1959, Mr Garfield Todd, the deposed Prime Minister of Southern Rhodesia, summed up the whole tragic situation and roundly blamed the white settlers for the part they had played. 'Of course,' he wrote, 'we Europeans are to blame to a large extent for the mistakes of the past five years, for we have not succeeded in implementing the policy of partnership simply because we have refused to face its implications.' On balance the European settlers have provided the mixture as before. Their exclusiveness, their charity and at the same time their bad manners all isolate them from the emerging African. They have maintained the mentality of conquerors while preaching the principles of partnership. They have failed to appreciate the extent to which they are seen as hypocrites. And as they know so little about the man who now confronts them in an increasingly menacing manner, they are in no position to take any effective remedial action.

CHAPTER 8

The Advanced Africans

The term 'advanced Africans' is one that is used by many European employers and by those responsible for the administration of African affairs to denote Africans who have raised themselves above their fellows to positions of responsibility at work, or to the leadership of trades unions or political parties. It is also used for those who occupy positions such as schoolteachers, priests, storekeepers and the like.

These advanced Africans, the emerging middle classes as they are sometimes called, are of course subject to the same environmental frustrations and bitterness as the African illiterates. They live in homes often as overcrowded, they are derided by the Europeans even more than are their less well-educated fellows, they are subject to similar pass restrictions. But their resentment and bitterness goes deeper because, in a more subtle way, they see the implications of the situation and its peculiar application in Central Africa. They know that people in other lands would accord them more respect and unlike the leaders of other proletariats, they do not have to delve back into the realms of long-past history for incidents upon which to base their hostility for the masters who dominate them.

The imposition of federation in 1953 is probably their greatest single disappointment. Most of them opposed it at the time and few have changed their minds since. Indeed, the public utterances of most European politicians gave them little alternative. They remember how Sir Roy Welensky said in the Northern Rhodesian Legislature in 1948 that 'the main reason why we need Federated States in Central Africa is because this will enable us to loosen the grip of the Colonial Office on the territory'. The implications of this remark was as clear to these Africans as was Sir Godfrey Huggins'—later Lord Malvern—comment at the opening of the Victoria Falls Conference called to discuss the possibilities of federation in 1949 that 'for some time to come Africans must be ruled by a benevolent aristocracy in the real sense of the term'. These and other similar utterances, many admittedly made for the benefit of the European electorate and not really intended for African ears, if indeed the speaker meant them at all, served, nonetheless to show the African élite that democracy was not for them—if the European politicians could help it. A bitter blow too, was when the final decision as to whether or not to federate was put to a vote in Southern Rhodesia. It could have been predicted with certainty that whatever Southern Rhodesians wanted would be unacceptable to Africans who look upon that territory as the real nigger in the woodpile, or, to transcribe the metaphor in more appropriate terms, the white bogeyman of Central Africa.

In an attempt to win over these hostile Africans, the minority of Africans it is true, but on the other hand, the only ones who really matter, there were promises of great economic benefits, to be enjoyed by all once the Federal State had got into its stride, of constitutional safeguards and even vague assurances of franchise reforms. A limited number of African members were elected to the Federal House, but in their election there was a large European vote so that few, if any, who were hostile to partnership were elected. In Northern Rhodesia and Nyasaland some Africans were also elected to the local assemblies.

There was just the hope that a liberal spirit might prevail in Southern Rhodesia with Mr Garfield Todd as Prime Minister and the African Affairs Board to keep watch for any discriminatory legislation. Yet both these hopes were groundless. Garfield Todd was discarded as being too liberal and the African Affairs Board was sidetracked the first time it made a real stand for African rights. To politically conscious Africans in Northern Rhodesia, the selection of Kariba rather than Kafue for the first great power scheme suggested a plot to bolster up the Southern Rhodesian white-dominated economy at the expense of Northern Rhodesia. Again, the action of the Northern Rhodesian European mine workers in asking the Southern Rhodesian and South African mine workers' unions whether they would be prepared to give assistance if required showed clearly that the Europeans of the north were determined to hold their positions even if it meant bringing in Southern Rhodesian or South African Europeans to help them.

The African middle classes feel very much more bitter over discriminating legislation than does the African proletariat. The ordinary African in the street does not like the rules and regulations that restrict his activities but he tends to accept them as part of the urban way of life. He knows no better.

Of recent years various apparently liberal measures have received much publicity. There was the opening of the Civil Service for Africans, the talk of multi-racial trades unions, the Apprenticeship Act that was at long last to open up new training facilities for Africans. But it was soon discovered that though the Civil Service could be technically open to all men there yet remained plenty of ways of overlooking those Africans who might possibly be suitable. Restrictive practices can still effectively prevent Africans taking on apprenticeships while the talk of multi-racial unions means very little when it remains possible for white unions to form separate branches within the union under the Industrial Conciliation Amendment Act and thus retain effective control of union policy.

There is absolutely nothing the African can legally do about all this. The Europeans often lecture him on what they are pleased to call the 'essential respect for law and order' but such phrases are anathema to a people who have no say in the framing of that law, who suffer discrimination at its hands both at home and at work and who have no facilities for altering it constitutionally. They are bitter about the charity of the Europeans and the way these same Europeans boast of the benefits they have provided for the African. European hypocrisy makes them especially bitter. So does the question of land. This is a subject about which they talk a great deal, not because they themselves are personally affected by it, but because it is a subject dear to the heart of every African not completely detribalized. Land is therefore always a good rallying cry for opening political speeches. In the early days, of course, not every African minded being shifted from the land he occupied. There was land to spare and most men were, in any case, used to shifting cultivation. But as the Africans of Southern Rhodesia see it there is now some 3,000 acres for every white farmer in the country and around six acres for every African. Worse still is the fact that when the new Land Husbandry Act is fully implemented a million Africans will be rendered landless, most of whom believe that under tribal law they possess certain communal land rights even though they do not care to exercise those rights until some future date.

Most of these disabilities cause more bitterness to the educated rather than to the uneducated African, to the politically conscious African rather than to the man who occupies little of his time pondering political issues. Yet it is this non-politically minded man whom right wing European journalists seem to meet and to quote as the 'average African'. It is true, of course, that there are a great many of these non-thinking Africans. But non-thinking does not imply non-feeling and even the non-politically minded African will begin to think—or feel—very deeply about politics if an African leader tells him in the right way that this is how he should think or feel. African leaders, indeed, do not require great histrionic ability or the capacity to move vast crowds with their oratory to incite the average African to turn on even those Europeans who have helped him and treated him well for years. Such a situation may smack of ingratitude, but when seen in perspective, the reason is not far to seek. Most of those who grew up in the towns, the leaders as well as the led, have been reared in conditions that give rise to every form of juvenile and adolescent delinquency. People in Britain know the effect that overcrowding, broken marriage, poverty, drunkenness and vice all have on growing children. The connection between these various influences and juvenile delinquency can be demonstrated in every European and American city. Yet the worst possible conditions imaginable in Britain would seem almost palatial if set alongside the conditions in which the average African urban child has grown up.

Surveys in Britain and elsewhere have also shown that juvenile crime is most marked where rich and poor live in relatively close proximity to each other and where the affluence of the one is clearly visible to the other. It is the same in Africa. To the bitterness that most Africans grow to feel at the social conditions in which they live is added the fact that to the educated African and also to a rather less extent to those who have had little or no schooling, the average European seems inordinately rich. An African schoolteacher once put into words how his people felt over this discrepancy. 'We are used to thinking of wealth in terms of cattle,' he began, 'and we say that a cow is worth £5. Now we know that every European owns one or even more cars, that he buys and sells houses costing many thousands of pounds, that in his house he has much priceless furniture and many fine clothes. If we add all this up it seems to us that every European has at least £10,000 worth of possessions and this means 2,000 cattle. This is an enormous herd for any man to own and if he has so many cows, why does he continue to work and to want more. Why does he need so much money, why is he so greedy that he does not give money away to the poor Africans?'

Reasoning of this kind is elementary and simple. But it is very telling when the African leader puts across such arguments to his people—in part because many of the leaders half believe it themselves.

The European attitude to these advanced Africans is a confusing one. In theory they are encouraged. It is felt that a middle class élite will set the same standard of conduct and stability that it does in European society. Most European employers and administrators therefore claim to be in favour of the emerging middle classes and to give them every encouragement. They forget that a middle class can be an extremely dangerous community if it is not handled aright for history shows that every successful revolution that has ever been mounted has been planned and organized by a frustrated or embittered middle class. And this is just the situation now to be found in Central Africa. Apart from the many disabilities to which these middle-class Africans are constantly subjected and to which reference has been made in previous pages, almost to the point of boredom, the African middle classes soon come to realize that their middle-class status seems only to be wanted and recognized at work. Here they are given responsibility, and their wages are often much in excess of their fellows. But for the sixteen hours of the day that they are not working they have to return to the community of people from whose ranks they have with so much difficulty risen and where the extra money in their pockets serves only to buy more beer, or an antique motor car that has more status value than mechanical worth.

In some instances, and in recent years only, attempts have been made to give better type houses to these middle-class Africans and in many cases these houses are set apart from the rest of the African community. But this is about the limit of the concessions made to them if one excludes the occasional room set aside in the beer hall and the fact that, in the last few years, they have been freed from obtaining the multitudinous passes carried by the average man, always provided they have with them at all times a pass to show that they do not need to carry passes.

None of these so-called advantages is very much of an incentive for these Africans to settle down and cultivate the virtues the Europeans believe to be inseparable from a middle-class group. The advanced Africans want to be different to their less well-educated or less able fellows and they want to be seen and recognized as different too, both by Africans themselves and by the Europeans as well. They want to live the kind of lives that Europeans live, enjoy the same privileges, and pastimes. When they travel in trains, go into hospitals, eat out or indeed whenever they find themselves in a situation outside their homes in which Africans are segregated or treated differently to Europeans, they want the treatment they receive to approximate more closely to that of the European than to that of the African. In hospitals, for example, they would like to have sheets, to which they have become accustomed, rather than the blankets which are believed to be all that Africans need. In trains, they would like to be served with the same courtesy that Europeans travelling in the same class as themselves are accorded. And if they can afford to eat in the better hotels, they would like to be able to go there.

The difficulties of these Africans do not end with their appearances in public. Behind the shutters of their homes they have other and in many ways as difficult problems to face. The vast majority of middle-class or advanced Africans are men. And theirs is domestically a lonely life, for only in the exceptional circumstances, where a man has found a wife with the same educational background as himself, can they hope to find the satisfaction out of monogamous marriages that the Church and many Europeans piously tell them to expect.

That the middle-class Africans are very alive to this problem of companionship in marriage was clear when I once asked forty of them to set out on paper the qualities they would most desire in a wife. I hoped that the answers would give some indication of how far the qualities felt to be important in tribal society were still rated highly. The replies listed a large number of qualities though many of them were variants of the same general idea. Thus 'respectful to visitors' and 'cheerful to strangers' were two that were very similar and that reflected the basic tribal attitude towards hospitality. These qualities were, however, not high on the list. The two most interesting aspects of replies was that beauty did not figure anywhere near the top and that the most popular reply was 'same education'. This was followed by domestic training and the ability to cook.

The majority of men who replied to the question were married to women of considerably lower educational qualifications to themselves. Further individual questioning showed that these men had succeeded for the most part in maintaining the higher standard of living they sought but that it was generally a lonely and unsatisfying experience living at so different a level to that of their wives. Yet the desire to have a wife who could be expected to enjoy the same things as themselves was expressed with the full recognition that considerable financial sacrifices would be entailed if such a mate could be found. They fully recognized that those few women who have moved closer to the European way of life than the majority could be expected to demand more money for diet, hygiene and appearance and that considerable inroads into the family budget would thereby be entailed.

Marriages between two people of roughly similar education and outlook are extremely few and far between, and the average middle-class African is in an unenviable position. His wife does not understand him or appreciate his difficulties—her own position must in another way be equally lonely—while most Europeans he meets in the course of his work are frankly hostile and frequently contemptuous into the bargain. Yet these Africans who have striven hard to raise themselves cannot help continuing to strive. And one of the things they seek more than almost anything else is some form of recognition, some means of achieving prestige that everyone must have in some measure. This they achieve in strange ways since none of the more normal forms are available to them. Thus, when in the presence of Europeans they will talk in English to those Africans near them to draw attention to themselves. The somewhat exotic clothes that many of them adopt are in the same way a means of attracting attention. So too are the refrigerators in their homes—in most cases these appliances cannot work because there is no electric power available— and often one sees small articles of furniture or decoration set up in the house with the price tags still affixed. This seeking after recognition by the acquisition of status possessions is carried to an excess not known in other communities and one of the first victims are the children. Most of the really bad cases of malnutrition in the urban areas occur in these better-to-do families and not amongst the really poor. This fact is very rarely recognized when the plight of urban children is in discussion and the remedy is obviously very different from that usually propounded.

Just as many of these people seek social recognition in strange out of the way forms, so too do they have to find unusual ways of employing their energy and their talents, that because of racial discriminations and the workings of the economic colour bar, many of them cannot utilize to the full during working hours. Some men find an outlet in joining social or political organizations. Others start societies, trade unions or political parties on their own. Most men when questioned will rationalize their actions and state that they are working for the betterment of their own people. This is no doubt true as far as it goes. There is no doubt, however, that they are also working for their own peace of mind even though they may not be aware of the fact. One man indeed who was questioned on this point was found to be undertaking simultaneously a whole variety of community activities that included acting as chairman of a welfare society, a burial society and a co-operative; he also held the secretaryship of his local denominational society and assistant secretaryship of his tribal group in the town. In his working hours this man kept the time-books of his employers' factory and answered to the call of 'boy' from his immediate European superior, an extremely uncouth and unpleasant individual in every way.

In Europe we would question the intention, even the honesty of a man actively working for the interests of the workers in a trade union and co-operative organizaton, for the aristocracy in the Kings of Matabeleland Memorial Society and for the Church in the Tabasinduna Presbytery. Such interests are much too devious to have a common purpose unless sublimation is accepted as the main motive.

Other men go into trade. This is a most important group of Africans whose value to the community both black and white is unhappily not recognized. These men are important because they are the only Africans who are economically independent of the European and they are also important because virtually none of those who are working up small businesses on their own account trouble to join political parties or even interest themselves in politics. Some African politicians may well go into trade to eke out a living outside the very precarious field in which they normally operate. But these exceptions apart, opportunities of working on their own seem to appeal more to Africans than working to drive the Europeans from their country.

Considering the limited opportunities that exist for individual development outside the European economy, it is quite remarkable just how many varied trading outlets have appeared. Many men trade from their homes. These include people who keep small stores of groceries available for sale to their neighbours; others are gardeners, snuff makers, public letter writers, watch repairers, sign writers, hair cutters, well sinkers, bus owners and photographers.

Most of the trade is done from shops. Some of these shops have been constructed by the Africans themselves although the vast majority have been rented from the local municipality or possibly from Indians or European landlords. The shops include all the usual kinds of retail outlets normally found in an urban area such as grocers, carpenters, tailors, watch and cycle repairers, hair cutters, butchers, cobblers and people dealing in firewood.

Much of this trading is illegal in the strict sense of the term for few of those who earn their living in this way trouble to take out the General Dealer licenses that the law demands. Even fewer of them could comply with the regulations requiring the keeping of books and accounts in the English language. Fortunately, the authorities turn a blind eye to this flaunting of the law. Otherwise there would be very few Africans trading at all.

They are a varied group of people who set up shop in one form or another. A few are well-educated men who have forsaken schoolmastering or clerical work for the potentially higher income of the trader. These are exceptions, however, and most of the men and women keeping shops have not even completed a primary education.

Very few shopkeepers make as much money as they could and the general level of shopkeeping is extremely low. Stocks are usually limited and badly arranged. In the grocery shops in particular, there is little or no order with goods and produce piled up on the floor or scattered about in a most haphazard manner. Dirt and untidiness prevail.

Much of this inefficiency can be variously attributed to the Africans' traditional attitude to the acquisition of wealth, coupled with the restricted avenues available for utilizing or investing money, to the many calls made upon the individuals' generosity by relations and friends, to laziness and finally to lack of education and experience of commercial practice.

The kind of overheads that a European would look for in an assessment of the Africans' trading costs are not high. Rents charged by municipalities are extremely low although the Indians usually ask a figure that takes some account of the potential value of the shop. But there are a variety of overheads that are never met in European society that load the shop with a considerable burden. Foremost amongst these are subsidies to relatives or friends. Most shopkeepers state that they give members of their family long-term credit that is rarely ever repaid. Many also employ their relatives in the shop, sometimes paying them in cash and sometimes in kind. Almost always these people are allowed to take whatever they need and they are usually accommodated free in the owner's house or they sleep in the shop. The general situation was summed up by one African grocer who said 'As a matter of fact I work in order that my relatives should not suffer'.

It is not an uncommon sight to see a shopkeeper sitting talking to friends outside his shop and taking no notice of customers who come to make a purchase. In the circumstances ruling such behaviour is not as illogical as it would seem. The shopkeeper takes the view that the shop is provided for his benefit rather than for the benefit of the community as a whole. In European society these two interests are closely inter-related, and self interest can best be furthered by service to the community. In the African community, however, hard work only produces cash that cannot buy any of the things that are worth having, but only a host of begging relatives. As the prestige value of generosity has little of its traditional recognition in the urban areas, there is virtually no incentive to betterment.

Many tradesmen take out insurance policies against fire and theft. The premiums seldom exceed 30s a year and the owners of the shops are usually prepared to display their certificates of insurance at the slightest provocation. Rather more secret are the charms that they use to attract customers to the shop. Africans in other walks of life say that few shopkeepers do without these charms although few of them would admit to using such devices when questioned by a stranger. Dealers in charms state that shopkeepers and hawkers are amongst their best customers. The most usual charm is a paste that is made with the fat of a white goat (for purity), the nest of the honeybird (because the bird leads men to honey) and ground-up particles of gum that exudes from certain trees. Quantities of this material are purchased for 6d or 1s and a small amount is burnt in the shop each day. A 6d lump was said to last for about a week. One hawker, a man of some education and a lay preacher for the London Missionary Society each Sunday, stated that these charms were indispensable for the successful operation of his business.

Lack of education is a serious obstacle to real progress in the trading field. Obviously sales ability does not necessarily correlate with scholastic attainment, but a rudimentary knowledge of the three Rs does help a man to keep a daily record of his sales, take stock from time to time, cost his assistants' labour and estimate adequate profit margins. Some Africans have developed ingenious means of overcoming their educational shortcomings. Carpenters who have never received any schooling at all have developed simple ways of working out the mathematics that carpenters must use in a variety of situations. Even those who cannot read are yet able to add in a simple manner by using their fingers, while to multiply they merely add the items the requisite number of times. They do, however, find some difficulty in estimating what a job will cost. Thus one one occasion, a tailor was seen putting a large patch on a pair of trousers. His price for this was 7s 6d and it appeared that this was the most he could extract from the customer after protracted bargaining. Careful measurements made of the cloth actually being used and the time taken to sew it on indicated that the cost of the repair should have been in the vicinity of 15s, a figure that greatly shocked the tailor concerned.

For all the inefficiency of the average shopkeeper, there are few insolvencies. This unusual situation derives from the fact that there is an extremely large number of potential customers to every shop and so there is only limited competition. The high prices that most Africans charge for their goods is yet a second reason for their remaining in business. In few cases are the prices charged by Africans to Africans lower than the amounts charged by European or Indian traders in the same town. Then too, few of the hawkers, who sell most of the fruit and vegetables, possess scales. They either buy small quantities of stock from European or Indian stores in town at retail rates and add a few pence to the cost price, or they purchase a sack of produce wholesale. But lacking the arithmetical ability to work out a fair selling price of these goods in small quantities, they usually err on the high side.

Much the same system of pricing is found in the majority of shops. The average shopkeeper's capital is limited and he purchases only small quantities of stock, again often at retail rates, and soaps, tinned foods, matches and soft drinks are sold at a few pence above prices ruling in European shops. Even branded goods are similarly overpriced. In the few larger African grocery stores prices are on a par with those elsewhere because the owners can purchase their stock wholesale and generally on more advantageous terms.

A feature of all Africans' trading is the use of 3d as a basic unit. Oranges may be retailed at two or three for 3d rather than at 1d or $1\frac{1}{2}$d. each, and the offer to purchase a penny-worth is usually refused. Only in the case of the more expensive cigarettes are sales at 1d each habitually recorded.

Few traders when questioned on this matter of higher prices attempt to justify them on the grounds that they are subject to excessive pilferage, that they must needs make an undue number of gifts or that their lack of education precludes their keeping proper control of the shop. Many of the men admitted quite openly that their charges were higher than those ruling in town and they justified their mark-up on the grounds of convenience. They pointed out that the public could walk into the European town if they chose but that by shopping in the African areas they were saving time and shoe leather.

The Advanced Africans   151

On the whole African traders are the most contented group of people in the urban areas. Yet, ironically, it is those who are most successful who tend to be the least contented. This is because there is usually a limit to their capacity to expand and this limit is European imposed. It either takes the form, common in many of the municipalities, of restricting the size of shops and not permitting a man to rent more than one, or, as is often the case around the large mining compounds, trading rights are given to Europeans who have both the cash and the skill to develop their ventures and thus limit the opportunities available to the Africans. While the majority of municipal councils continue to be dominated by Europeans who are themselves in trade, this latter difficulty is unlikely to be resolved.

It is not, of course, every African who wants to trade or who has whatever attributes are necessary to make such activity profitable. Men who, for one reason or another, do not attempt to improve their standards of living by using their initiative on their own account make vigorous, though generally unskilful attempts to readjust the balance of power between themselves and the Europeans by collective activities of various kinds. Such collective behaviour is by no means novel to those fresh from a tribal context, while men and women born in town or those who have lived long in a westernized environment, have learnt by bitter experience of the power of the well-organized and single-minded European façade that so successfully controls and limits their activities.

African collective reaction to social and economic conditions comprises three forms of self-help organization. In the first place there are the societies and clubs designed for purely personal ends such as burial societies and collective insurance schemes to cover unemployment or train journeys home. These types of organizations are by far the most numerous but they are remarkable more for their widespread nature and variety than for any real value they bestow on the community.

Pursued with rather less vigour, though generally with more success, because the objectives are less complex, are the recreational societies, clubs and groups that have no self-preservative motif. Finally there are the organizations that aim to unite the African people, to raise their standard of living as a community or to provide a common front against European domination. This group includes the African separatist churches, the trades unions, co-operative societies and political parties.

In Southern Rhodesia, any society, organization or club that desires official recognition must register its existence with the Native Commissioner. Registration consists of submitting two copies of the organization's constitution to the Native Department. One is filed in the department—if the object of the organization is considered suitable or desirable—and the second is returned to the organization with the department's stamp affixed to signify approval and registration.

Organizations that, for one reason or another, feel that the stamp of government approval is desirable, make quite sure that whatever their real objectives or political aspirations, nothing but high-sounding phrases couched in language that is intended to please and to dispel any suspicion are included in the constitution submitted to the Native Department for approval and recognition. Such patriotic sentiments as 'To co-operate at all times with government in the peaceful administration of native affairs' occur in numerous constitutions filed in the Native Department offices, while frequently included in the so-called rules of the organization are such phrases as 'Any member who fails to pay his annual tax shall be expelled from the society'.

Whether the organizations claim, either publicly or in the copy of their constitution that is submitted to the Native Department, to exist for economic, recreative or community purposes, they all have an underlying and seldom publicized political intent. In the last resort this political bias is understandable. The urban Africans' unhappy personal situation is what it is for political reasons. His lowly economic position, his poverty, his lack of cultural opportunities, the limits placed upon his opportunities for personal advancement and his social insecurity are all due to political factors and to the political domination of the white race. That his economic or self-help organizations, his trades unions and even, to some extent, his cultural or sporting organizations, should be heavily, though for obvious reasons disguisedly, tinged with a political flavour is understandable and to be expected.

The Europeans see clearly that so long as the African is unable to help himself he will remain an extremely expensive burden on the taxpayer. But it is equally clearly recognized that once Africans learn to take care of themselves and to stand on their own feet, there is no telling how far this new-found ability may impinge on European interests and so-called rights. Official assistance or encouragement to African organizations is accordingly lukewarm at best, while private European individuals, who act as advisors, are looked upon askance by the majority of their white fellows.

Welfare societies of various kinds have existed for many years. As early as 1933, the Africans in Northern Rhodesia formed a Native Welfare Organization whose aim was to safeguard the rights and interests of the natives of Northern Rhodesia. At that time, interests were not seen predominantly in political terms, although quite early on there were motions from the Africans asking government assistance in the matter of the European habit of elbowing Africans off pavements!

The Advanced Africans

Most common of the purely welfare organizations are the burial societies. Africans, even those who have lived all their lives in town, are, like their tribal forbears, particularly concerned that burial should be carried out in a properly prescribed manner. Indeed, Africans come closer to the European way of life in their funerals than they ever do during their lives. They have hearses, coffins draped with flowers and all the expensive paraphernalia of a Victorian funeral whenever they, or the society to which they have donated weekly contributions, can afford it. The fees of these societies are moderate and rarely exceed 2s 6d a month. Most burial societies augment their funds by running periodic dances and with the accumulated monies they have obtained they offer an elaborate range of assurance. In addition to a fine burial, they offer assistance when in economic distress, free train fares home, unemployment relief, assistance in meeting rents and also various sickness benefits.

Needless to say these ambitious objectives are rarely realized. The funds usually prove totally inadequate even if the office-bearers refrain from draining the slender resources to their own advantage.

In the majority of organizations designed to afford economic or social security there is a tribal or a territorial basis, and members are usually recruited from the same tribe or country of origin. The fact that all members frequently come from the same tribe also serves to give to such societies a stabilizing rôle in upholding traditional practices and regulating the conduct of members in their day-to-day activities.

Although few self-help societies survive more than a few years, and fewer still give value for money, it would be wrong to write them off as so much waste of energy on the part of the office-bearers and a financial loss to the members. The experience that the officials gain, and that the members gain of these African officials, is of considerable long-term value, even if its immediate benefits appear very limited. While it is true that the majority of subscribers lose their money, they are little worse off in the long run. They may not receive the burial they desire and they may have to vacate their homes because assistance with the rent has not materialized. But they are making a contribution to the evolutionary development of the African that is fundamental and that could come from no other source. Self-help does not solely relate to material benefits. It provides training in honesty, administration and self-reliance, and the funds subscribed in the early days provide a training ground in organization and financial control that is fundamental if the African people are ever to aspire to parity with the Europeans.

A second kind of organization is the sporting or recreational society. These include football, boxing, tennis, dancing, singing and music clubs. These organizations are more viable than the economically inclined organizations as they make fewer calls upon members' pockets; they meet more frequently and thus retain a greater concentration of interest in their activities. Some, however, endeavour to provide funds for burial and other contingencies and so resemble the economic organizations to a limited extent. Funds for such purposes are raised by means of dances or receipts arising from the particular type of activity of the society or club concerned.

Strangest of the organizations that aim to unite the African people against the Europeans are the various religious movements, in part Christian and in part something more primitive. The inspiration for this movement springs largely from the educated Africans who see very clearly how great is the difference between Christian preaching and practice. Even the missionaries are seen to have their own special ideas on Christianity for Africans and Christianity for Europeans. The advanced Africans do not know a great deal about Christianity for Europeans because in very few churches do African and European Christians attend the same service. It is apparent to most Africans, however, that the church-going section of Europeans is very small. And as, under present circumstances, religion for Africans means largely going to Church, they feel the Europeans can no longer be sincere in their desire to spread the Gospel.

They see and come in contact with a great deal of Christianity for Africans. To many of them this is little more than another means of maintaining the present *status quo* between the races and keeping the African in a lowly position. After many years of contact with Europeans, the Africans have learnt that the African Christian is all too often looked upon by the whites as a hypocrite or a 'spoiled nigger'. There is little idea anywhere that he has become a brother in Christ. Indeed, Africans have for the most part long lost respect for the European missionary who preaches on Sunday that the strong should care for the poor. They see too many of their own kind exploited for six days of the week by self-confessed Christians to find anything but hypocrisy in the present European-sponsored Christian quest for the African soul.

Three courses are open to such Africans. They can become atheists, they can join one of the entirely African Separatist churches or they can begin to wonder whether something of the old African religion could not be re-created in a modern guise. How many of these men are actually atheists is not known. If religion is defined as 'The facing of the unknown', it is unlikely that there will be many amongst present-day urban Africans, irrespective of their education or training.

Few intelligent Africans care to join the African Separatist churches at the present time. Membership is small, there is little prestige or glamour in joining but usually only a lot of organizational work. It remains for the majority of these men to continue dissatisfied Christians or else seek an answer to their spiritual needs in the old religion of the past. This latter development has already begun and several educated men have expressed the hope that at a future date M'limo[1] would once again command the obedience and respect of the African people. Even ordained African ministers are not too antagonistic to this cult and it would seem that separatism from the Christian Church into some form of different, possibly ancestral, religion is not far distant from the minds of even the most devout.

This harking back to the earlier all-African form of belief is also encountered in the urban areas of the Union of South Africa, where, as in Rhodesia, it is due to two main factors. In the first place there is the growing sense of national unity amongst the intelligentsia and the consequent need for some symbol that is purely African and that will transcend national boundaries and tribal differences. In the second place it is due to the deep-seated sense of insecurity which the majority feel as a result of the little understood stresses and strains of an urban life so dominated by discriminatory legislation that to the African is the antithesis of Christianity.

The development of these various African self-help organizations has taken a clearly defined path. The early welfare societies, with their often political slant, gave way gradually to more industrially motivated movements and the trade unions that gradually emerged, usually illegally in the early days, were a quite logical consequence of the social and industrial conditions ruling in the urban areas. That certain groups should come into being to limit industrial exploitation in one way or another is as natural as that others should attempt to provide facilities for adequate burial. In neither case can the African achieve satisfaction as an individual, and the formation of new groups to deal with new problems is understandable. That the first African trade union in Southern Rhodesia to call its members out on strike grew directly out of the Bantu Benefit Society, an organization created to help African railway employees in cases of financial difficulty, serves to place the African trades unions in their right perspective. They are not isolated instances of African solidarity or examples of borrowing or attempting to impose alien and revolutionary creeds, as is frequently suggested. They are part and parcel of the native peoples' whole reaction to urban and industrial conditions, a reaction that every other similarly placed racial group has shown in similar circumstances. Trades unions formed under such

[1] To many Africans south of the Zambesi, the God M'limo, who is believed to live in the Matopo hills in Matabeleland has never really been discredited. Emissaries of his cult are still found in all parts of Southern Rhodesia and his name is known and venerated in areas as distant as Bechuanaland and Portuguese East Africa.

conditions are not necessarily any more anti-European than are the burial societies or the dance clubs. They come into being merely to protect the Africans' own interests in the industrial sphere, as other organizations help in the social sphere, and because no other organization is capable of providing the necessary help. That they subsequently acquire an anti-white bias is due to the manner in which they are treated more than to any inherent political hostility. The African is no student of industrial history and he does not have to be. His experience is that of every other proletariat that has preceded him in the same rôle. He has tried and failed with single-handed negotiations and he has no confidence in the efforts of those who claim to champion his cause. He uses them when he feels they can be useful, but his whole way of life, the conditions of everyday existence and his prospects in the urban area are a living witness of the failure of these forms of negotiation. He has come to realize, by the same path, what the nineteenth century British labourer came to realize, that salvation must depend upon his own resourcefulness and upon his co-operation with others of the same colour and in the same position as himself. Even his relatively recent industrial experience has taught him that strength can only be answered by strength and that negotiations that are conducted from positions of weakness are inevitably unsuccessful.

It is impossible to say exactly how many Africans are members of trade unions, for the records are seldom accurate and membership is often short term. Migrant workers never make good union members in any country and the African labour force is still predominantly migrant in character. But, as a general rule, it is clear that the trade union movement, ably assisted both by the trade union movement in Great Britain, the Colonial Office and in some instances by employers' organizations themselves, is fast replacing tribalism as the rallying point for African solidarity. Its inter-tribal basis is also speeding up the acceptances of the wider concept of African nationalism. It is, therefore, at once an organization in the direct evolutionary line leading to political parties. Indeed in the special circumstances applicable in Central Africa, the leaders of the one are largely also the leaders of the other. It is not surprising, therefore, that trade unions have focused their attention on matters far transcending industrial relations or the questions of adequate conditions of service. They have been chosen by the African as the most suitable weapon with which to attack white domination and they are, therefore, of necessity very political in outlook. This choice is logical enough in the Africans' situation where the two sides of industry represent, to all intents and purposes, the two races. Africans see clearly enough that the European-dominated economy, geared as it is to low African wages, is at its most vulnerable on the industrial front, and of course all the economic discrimination to which they are subject is imposed on them by the European voter in the legislative programme of his political party.

One must agree with much of what the most virulent critics say of the African trade union movement; and also of its leaders. Records are usually unreliable, there is frequent misuse of union funds, and leadership is often motivated by individual ambition rather than industrial or even political factors. But is there a country that can boast of trade union leadership completely free from such faults? There must always be good and bad trade union leaders and on balance the African movement has accounted itself well and with a proper sense of responsibility. Certainly the two major unions, the African Railway Workers' Union in Southern Rhodesia and the African Mineworkers' Union in Northern Rhodesia have repeatedly been complimented by successive Commissions of Enquiry on their moderation and their sense of responsibility at times when their white counterparts were panicking into the most unethical trade union practices. Thus, when the Southern Rhodesian African Railway workers brought their members out on strike for the first time in 1945, their behaviour was favourably commented upon by both the subsequent Commissions of Enquiry and by the Government. The behaviour of the Europeans, on the other hand, who had long denied that Africans should be allowed to strike because they would not understand the ethics of the weapon, showed that they had much to learn in the field of industrial negotiation. Speaking of this strike, the Tredgold Commission commented, 'Africans were to be told in peremptory terms that all who did not return to work would be dismissed with loss of all long-service privileges. No protection was promised to those who were prepared to resume. In this, as in most strikes, some at least were not willing strikers, but acting under compulsion. We consider that it is both unfair and unwise to order a return to work under threat of instant dismissal until full arrangements have been made to ensure that those who obey this order are protected against the possible consequences of obeying it.'

The experience of negotiation with African trades unions in Northern Rhodesia is the same. Following negotiations for better conditions of service in the copper belt in 1950, the Commission of Enquiry was able to report, 'Throughout negotiations African union officials conducted themselves in a highly responsible manner, showing high negotiating qualities which earned them the compliments of the general manager and conciliator.' And this pattern has been maintained along similar lines ever since. Indeed, the Africans see in the irresponsible behaviour of their European counterparts the seeds of their ultimate defeat and one African, Mr John Banda of the African National Congress summed up the attitude of his people in the words, 'We Africans know that if a beast is dying it kicks out. So you don't go near it—you stand away and let it die.' Increasingly Africans leaders are becoming aware that they only have to stand away and let European folly and world opinion complete their task for them.

Yet the task of these African leaders is far from easy. In the first place, there is the difficulty of convincing their members that time is so much on their side that even patience will not be long extended. Then there is a second battle that they must win and this is as much with themselves as it is with controlling their members. They know very well that if they play their hands reasonably well they cannot lose. But emotionally they are driven by a deep sense of personal humiliation and bitterness that tends frequently to inhibit clear thinking. Moreover, they face certain immediate problems that are not normally found in industrial societies. 'In Africa,' as Miss Marjorie Perham has pointed out, 'the general quiescence and passivity of the tribally divided masses under foreign rule has meant that leaders have arisen to create a movement rather than a movement has created a leader. The principal emotional driving force among African leaders is their individual battle against an inferiority of status as a member of a race and not of a nation, and their sense of humiliation upon realizing their own retarded position among the people of the world. The new leader has to build his own platform and jump upon it and built it in the main of imported materials. He must keep up the interest and emotion of the masses by belligerency and he cannot afford to be moderate.'[1]

None of this makes the task of the African leaders any easier. And the situation is further complicated, for, were they to agree with the policy of the Southern Rhodesian Government they would have to relinquish their leadership and leave the handling of African Affairs to the white electorate. And in Northern Rhodesia the official policy is one of partnership which the African leaders and their followers are determined to resist since they still want the paramountcy of the Devonshire Declaration.

To oppose the official view is to court disaster and is, therefore, to say the least, fraught with certain hazards in both territories, as those who have been arrested and held without trial know to their cost. Yet increasingly, and often against their better judgement, African leaders are being driven to resort to violence.

From the African point of view, there is much to justify this development. In the first place there is no other way. It is all very respectable for the Southern Rhodesian Minister of Justice to condemn the African National Congress as he did before the Beadle

[1] Marjorie Perham, 'The Psychology of African Nationalism', *Optima*, March 1960.

Inquiry in 1959, stating that 'the purpose of the Congress was to excite disaffection towards the Constitution with the object of altering the constitution by unlawful means.'[1] But the Southern Rhodesian Africans have no constitutional means of ventilating their views or even influencing the situation. Constitutonal safeguards have not given them the protection that was anticipated, and in all three territories the use of boycotts and strikes has proved of no avail. Thus, in 1953 the African Congress had organized boycotts against butcher shops that sold 'boys meat' containing mostly bone and unsaleable offal. When the African leaders of the boycott were arrested and brought to trial on charges of malicious conspiracy, it was shown that their Urban Advisory Council had tried for over two years to discuss the matter reasonably with the local European Chamber of Commerce but that their request had been continuously stalled.

Power is either force or it is votes. Denied the votes, it is hard to see how anybody would not come in due course to rely on the former. In this reliance the Africans have plenty of European examples to follow. In 1949 Sir Roy Welensky had warned the British Government that if they persisted in their policy of African paramountcy the Europeans would challenge this policy by force. He went on to warn the Colonial Secretary that in the last resort he would not hesitate to appeal to Southern Rhodesia and the Union of South Africa for support. And on many subsequent occasions the term 'force' has fallen from the lips of this bellicose Prime Minister when he has seemed not to be having everything his own way. To the Africans, such threats to use force are no less unconstitutional than are the threats that they are increasingly beginning to utter, while the presence of an armed police force enforcing an unpopular discriminatory legal system is, in African eyes, itself a permanent and ever visible resort to force.

The final argument, as the African leaders view the situation, is that force pays off. Force has proved the only means of ridding other lands of despots, as the revolutionaries of France, Britain and America have all in turn discovered. It has served to hasten independence in many parts of the Commonwealth. It unquestionably furthered Nyasaland's constitutional development. In Northern Rhodesia most adult Africans can remember how, before they were organized into unions, they were brushed aside during the war years when they sought improved conditions. A Commission of Enquiry had revealed that in 1940 many of their grievances were very real. Wages were, in fact, lower than they had been in the early 1930's. Yet they obtained no redress from the copper companies and their demonstrations were broken up with tear gas. The well-organized European

[1] Report of the Review Tribunal (Preventitive Detention Temporary Provision Act, 1959).

miners on the other hand, who had, by threatening strike action at a time when copper was in desperate need by the Allies, held both the companies and Britain to ransom, were given extra pay increases and assurances for their long-term security that were extremely unfair to the Africans. A long sequence of such incidents prompted Mr Chipembare, a Nyasaland political leader to remark:

> 'Anything like moderation will never get us anywhere . . . the only language which British imperialism can understand is the language of extreme conflict.'

This may be an extreme view, but there is undoubtedly some truth in it. There can be no question, however, but that at the present time and in their present predicament, force is favoured as a political weapon by many Africans who have become increasingly embittered at European delaying tactics and hypocrisy. They see no other way; they see their masters resorting to it and they know that every other race has used it successfully when faced with a situation similar to their own. If force is a 'reversion to type' as Europeans are prone to remark whenever an African raises the question of violence, then it is a reversion to a basically human type and not just a black-skinned one.

Many people in Britain can grudgingly understand the Africans' resort to force even if they are sorry to see it happen. But what they cannot understand is the brutality that Africans often show to their own people at such a time. During the Mau Mau trouble in Kenya there were frequent examples of the murder of Africans, while in Central Africa, those Africans who side with the Europeans or who favour a policy of gradualism are often threatened and sometimes physically ill-treated.

Yet the reason for such actions is not far to seek. They have their cause in the deep-seated sense of humiliation, frustration and bitterness that the politically-awakened African feels. That he should declare war on the present set-up is understandable and surely just as understandable is his hostility to anybody who remotely intervenes in the interest of the *status quo*. And some pro-European Africans go a great deal further than passive acceptance of the situation. These are the people whom African nationalists cannot tolerate at any price. Their fury is understandable when they say 'I can forgive a European who discriminates against me because he does it out of ignorance, but I cannot forgive an African who supports the theory that Europeans are justified in discriminating against the African'. To an African trade unionist or nationalist politician any co-operation with the Europeans is as much treasonable as was the behaviour of the Vichy Government in France to the Maquis and to the Free French Movement fighting outside France. One can, perhaps, understand the feelings of these Africans and perhaps even their violent reactions, when they hear a Northern Rhodesian African Member of the Federal Parliament speak of the Prime Minister, Sir Roy Welensky, in the following words. 'I would like to say a word on the criticisms levelled on the leadership of the Hon. Prime Minister of the Federation. They do not really surprise me. Jesus Christ was crucified by men whom he came to save.'

Even as little as fifteen years ago, the educated African would have been happy to have entered European society on almost any terms. Now he has found his feet in another field and to that field the white men must one day soon come asking for terms. For the Europeans have lost the chance to talk to him even as equals. The African today has now no time for compromise for much the same reason that Britain had no time for compromise in the happy days of gun-boat diplomacy in the nineteenth century. To the African, the word compromise is only found in the political vocabulary of people no longer in the ascendant.

Above all, the African wants revenge. He wants to settle scores of long standing before embarking on Constitution making for the future. Whether there will still be Europeans in the Rhodesias when he has had his revenge is uncertain. It may be that once he attains power he will extract only a limited revenge—as the now all-powerful trades unions have taken of the employers in Britain today. Or will he follow the path of the Congo?

CHAPTER 9

The End of an Era

It is easy enough to say that the European settlers must come to terms with the Africans, accept them and their ways, and cease complaining about their apparently irrational ways of thought and action. Certainly they will have to change their behaviour quite drastically. But even the most drastic of changes will alone not prove sufficient if Central Africa is to look forward to a period of peaceful racial co-existence. European behaviour and attitudes have produced a whole set of now quite independent problems.

Seen objectively, there are three possible solutions for Central Africa. The settlers can maintain something approaching the *status quo* by force, or the Africans can gain control—again by force—and proceed to eject all or most of the Europeans after the manner of the Congo. The final possibility is that there could be a multiracial community, providing a fair living for people of every race on terms of normal equality.

Despite what some of the most die-hard settlers may think or say, the first possibility, the use of force by Europeans, could not ultimately succeed. For even if they were to win a straight test of strength with the Africans, the resulting chaos would make their lives quite unworthwhile living. The Africans, for their part, can much more easily survive in conditions of social and economic turmoil. Many of them have been living in conditions that are very little different for a number of years. But everything that in the past had made life so attractive for the Europeans, their freedom, their privileges, the luxury and the spaciousness, would have been lost forever.

A Congo approach with an African Government in complete ultimate control of the territory might satisfy some Africans for a time. But these Africans would soon find out, as their leaders already know, that they must depend for many years ahead on Europeans for their technical services and for the expansion of the economy. To drive them out of the country, as many of their fellows advocate, would bring no benefit to anybody and certainly reduce the possibility of Europeans being recruited from other countries to replace those who had left.

It is to the attainment of the third idea, the concept of a multiracial community, that most people subscribe and for which most of the proposals for a solution have been directed. Before looking at these proposals, however, it may be useful to attempt to formulate what are the essential requirements of any plan if it is to succeed. Such a

The End of an Era

plan must be devised to work in a specific case, not in a general one. It is no use proposing some formula whereby so many black men of such and such a level of education and sophistication can live alongside and share government with so many white people of a different level of education and attainment. Rather it has to provide a specific formula for Rhodesia whereby a majority of black men, who feel very bitter and who are in many cases also full of hate, can settle down to responsible and peaceful co-existence with a minority of Europeans many of whom feel only fear and prejudice against them. If this were not difficult enough, there are also other requirements. A workable plan must recognize that neither Africans nor Europeans have any confidence in the guidance or intervention of Britain in working out their future. The plan must also recognize that there are no individuals in Central Africa itself who enjoy even a modicum of goodwill on both sides. On a more domestic level it must also recognize that it will not be possible to turn Africans into Europeans in three generations and it must be able to convince Europeans willingly to forgo the privileges of the present time if they would have security in the future.

Any solution that recognizes all these various realities must of necessity contain economic, social and political provisions. In the circumstances, no approach that makes only a single recommendation is likely to succeed. Yet most of the proposals that are made are of such a kind. There are the people who see the answer in juggling with the franchise so as to ensure the maximum degree of African participation in Government conducive with a fair degree of responsibility. Other people see the answer in more and better housing and others again think that all will be well if Africans are given opportunities to advance to higher ranks in the Civil Service, industry and commerce.

Admirable though these various ideas—and many others like them—may be in themselves, alone they are unlikely to effect any real improvement. Perhaps the least effective of all is the approach of the constitutionalists, for in the absence of any means of measuring hate they could never hope to find a satisfactory franchise formula. Indeed, the African in his present mood has little time for the niceties of democratic government nor indeed for compromise proposals. He has the ball at his feet and it is a new and thrilling experience. In any case, it is of little use giving the African public responsibility if he continues to be subject to rudeness and abuse from Europeans as a private citizen. In the same way, there is no point in seeking the solution in better housing if there is to be no opportunity for individual men and women to better themselves; or to create openings in the Civil Service and in industry if the educational programme is to lag behind.

OMS—L*

It is a total approach that is wanted and the only satisfactory solution is one that will do a great many things quickly and all at the same time. To achieve this total approach will require enormous financial resources and an impartial body of people able to assist both races as may be necessary and at the same time protect the legitimate interests of either race that may be threatened.

It is not particularly difficult to list the things that need to be done. And it is clear that no single remedial action has any special priority over any other. Many people might suggest that an end to all privilege based upon race would be the most urgent prerequisite to better race relations and there is much to commend this belief. Certainly race relations can never be normal until such measures are taken. But it is impossible to legislate against prejudice although it should be possible to make the overt expression of prejudice, either collectively or individually, at work or in the social or political fields, quite unworthwhile for the people concerned.

Privileges that are supported in law are in their way a form of collective bad manners, and bad manners, either collective or individual, will have to be rigorously condemned. The harm they can do far transcends their apparent insignificance. Thus, the Report of the National Convention published in 1960 commented, 'It is important to realize that even if it made little or no immediate change, the removal of the so-called pin-pricks is imperative for other reasons. They are to be condemned, not so much on account of the disability imposed, but because they contain an implied insult. It is an insult to declare the cinemas open to Asians and then declare that they sit separately. In so doing the European is implying that the Asian is not fit to sit next to him. If one signpost indicates "European ladies" and the other "non-European females" that is more than a pin-prick. It is a gross and unnecessary insult.

'It is bad enough when the insult is implied by some private organization, such as a turf club or cinema, but when it is enshrined in the law and supported by the refusal of the state to alter it, then the private insult becomes a public canker. That is why a national renunciation of social disabilities has become an urgent necessity.'

The complete relaxation of the colour bar and the end of European exclusiveness will be as difficult to attain in Central Africa as are the attempts being made by the Indian Government to end untouchability. Restaurants will have to open their doors to all races and there will have to be similar treatment given to Africans in shops, trains and hospitals as the Europeans enjoy. There is certainly little likelihood that Africans will either abuse those opportunities or reveal behaviour very different to that of the Europeans. Indeed, where the two races do happen to occupy common social facilities, such as in certain hotels in Northern Rhodesia, the Africans show very much more sense of decorum than do many copper belt miners away from the mine for a long weekend.

The attitude towards African leaders will also have to be radically altered and this applies more perhaps to Europeans in the upper ranks of government and the Civil Service than it does to the man in the street. African leaders will have to be treated with all the courtesy that is normally accorded to representatives nominated to negotiate by their rank and file. It may well be that some of these leaders will prove untrustworthy, or that others will have private lives that do not bear close inspection, that often they will exaggerate, distort the truth or misappropriate party funds. But integrity is not the only virtue in public life, and though one does not want to under-estimate its importance, it must be remembered that there are also other virtues and few individuals of any race possess them all in full measure. There is, for example, fair play, tolerance, sympathy and understanding, to mention only a few that are lacking in many of the settler leaders as well as in the average European settler.

Industry and commerce are in the forefront of any policy changes involving Africans, for it is at work that Africans and Europeans have their only worthwhile contacts. In practice two lines of action are needed here, obvious but neither easy to achieve. There is room for more legislation in the field of industrial relations and, secondly, there can and should be a greater degree of co-operation amongst European employers themselves in ensuring fair dealing and sound personnel policies.

The British system of industrial relations is based on the concept of voluntary agreement. We take the line that the less the government interferes in employer-union relations the better and the more likely the two sides are to work out a *modus vivendi*. We may be right. Other countries, Germany and India for example, regulate their industrial relations policies more closely. They take the view that the majority may be rather less responsible than the minority of either side and that to leave policy matters to the mercy of the majority is dangerous. So one finds in these countries legislation restricting the rights both of organized labour and organized management so as to ensure that the best interests of the community do not suffer if one side finds itself dominant.

How far should we be justified in suggesting legislation to limit trade union activity in Central Africa? Certainly it is not too late to lay down certain sanctions—sanctions that would have to limit both sides in one way or another. We could, for example, do what the T.U.C. in Britain recommended as policy for the re-birth of trade unionism in Germany after the war; that is, encourage specifically industrial unions to the exclusion of general or craft unions. Some people find this idea shocking. It is true that craft unions were the pioneers of unionism in Britain and that to permit men to organize how or where they will has an air both of tradition and of democratic procedure. But equally there is some merit in using the experience gained of trade union organization in Western European countries to avoid some of the pitfalls we have encountered ourselves. General unions, for example, have the inherent drawback of overworked secretaries busying themselves on behalf of dock labourers one day, farm workers the next, and perhaps concerning themselves with the problems of lorry drivers thereafter—none of which occupations may have been those in which they themselves grew up or of which they have any real working knowledge. Valuable though craft unions may have been in the old days of the guilds, there is no denying that in the twentieth century they are continually haunted by the threat of demarcation disputes. Industrial unions can avoid many of those difficulties. They have their own especial kinds of problem but the consensus of opinion is that they are the most adaptable to the needs of industry today.

Every encouragement—to the point even of legislation—could therefore be given to the setting-up of trade unions along industrial lines in Central Africa; and it is probable that the majority of responsible people, both black and white, would agree with such a step. Some employers are certainly doing all they can to assist Africans in the development of their trades unions. Usually these are the large international companies. But these large companies will suffer with the rest when trouble comes if they do not take more care to raise the general level of management in the smaller concerns around them and, above all, impress on these smaller brothers the need to recognize and treat with African trades unions. In fact, one can go further and say that it is all too often the larger and more liberal companies who are, under existing conditions, the first target for ambitious African trade union leaders, who know well enough that it is here that the easiest victories are won. Large companies have little, therefore, to be complacent about, however benevolent their own policies. The solidarity of employers, provided always that one of its first objectives is to raise the general level of management, is probably the surest way of inculcating into emerging African trades unions a sense not only of loyalty to their members but of responsibility in the demands they make.

Then there is the question of personnel managers. In countries where management and men are divided on racial as well as on the usual lines this is an especially vital rôle. Ideally, the personnel manager is outside the management hierarchy, acting as counsellor to both sides, interpreting, explaining and ensuring as far as he can that the actions and policies of management are fair and reasonable and seen so to be. The perosnal qualities that he needs above all are integrity and judgement. But all too often men are selected as personnel managers either because they know something about text-book techniques of personnel management or because they are familiar with African language and customs. Sometimes, even, they are put in the personnel department because nobody knows quite what to do with them anywhere else.

A knowledge of personnel management technique is not an essential pre-requisite for appointment. Far too much of a mystique has recently grown up round these techniques. They can be easily taught to the right person and, in any case, are little more than applied common sense. A knowledge of African language and custom is also far less necessary than in the past. The African industrial worker is coming to resemble more and more his western counterpart. The personnel manager in Africa today should therefore be a man who has learned as much about personnel problems and labour attitudes in western society as he knows of African tribal society and tribal ways. In fact, if he appears to know too much about tribal society, he is often branded by the Africans as a reactionary who will hold back the clock—the same attitude, alas, as the urban African often takes to the anthropologist.

Good personnel managers will be invaluable in helping to break down the attitude of many European employers who look upon trades unions in general and African unions in particular as 'the enemy'. Such an idea disappeared in Europe in the 1930's. And it must disappear very quickly in Africa if African trades unions, knowing as they do how trades unions are treated in more enlightened countries, are to retain a semblance of respect for the white people with whom they negotiate.

Yet another essential is for industry to start training Africans for the lower and middle ranks of management even if this involves, for a time at least, a reduction in the overall efficiency of the company. On the day that the first African becomes a director of a British public company in Africa, the settlers will have achieved a breakthrough comparable to the flight of Major Gagarin into space. No time should be lost in attempting such a move. A start might indeed be made by one of the two great copper mining groups of Northern Rhodesia. Had Mr Lawrence Katilungu not been killed in a car crash towards the end of 1961 he would have been an ideal candidate for such an appointment.[1]

Then there is the whole question of wages, charity, material humanitarianism. For so long now low wages and expensive social services have been the established practice that people in Central Africa have come to regard them as part and parcel of the African

[1] Lawrence Katilungu was for many years General Secretary of the African Mineworkers Union.

way of life, the price the European has to pay for African inefficiency and the long drawn-out process of detribalization. Coupled with this linking of low wages and subsidized services has been the tendency to lay far too much store on the material aspects of humanitarianism. If footballs and playing fields, good housing and adequate facilities for keeping the body clean have been provided, the settlers have felt no further obligation to their African employees. In point of fact, it matters far less that there should be bad housing, limited facilities for washing or recreation than that the morale of the individuals should be in good shape. I do not want to minimize the importance of good housing but only to suggest that it is not an end in itself. Indeed, if other measures are not taken it is not even a beginning.

Morale is bolstered by self-respect and human dignity, not by the possession or enjoyment of material goods. If it were, there could never be enough houses, never enough footballs, never enough motor cars. The trend in Central Africa has been that both body and soul have been degraded. Nobody has shown the African any humanity. Nobody has done very much for him as a man. Even material advantages have been restricted, well below the level found in the Union of South Africa.

A general increase of wages for all grades of African would have considerable advantages to the entire economy. There would doubtless be some immediate unemployment as European employers sifted out the good workers from the bad. But such a trend would be only temporary. If, as wages were raised, all economic colour bars were also lifted and a serious start was made to give Africans better training facilities as well as to liberalize the opportunities available for them to enter trade, two things would follow very quickly. In the first place, there would be an early increase in the number of African entrepreneurs who would quickly absorb the currently unemployed. Secondly, there would be an acceleration of economic activity that would go far to reduce the need for subsidized housing, education and health services.

A frustrated middle class is something that no community can afford for any length of time and the emerging African middle class have been frustrated from the start. They will have to be especially wooed. Opportunities for trade as well as for development in professional, technical and managerial posts will of course follow from the relaxation of economic colour bars. But these alone will not be enough. Such people need respect and social recognition, not patronage, and to achieve the first two without the last will not be easy. But the example of other countries is sufficient warning of the dangers to be met.

In India the educated middle classes were a British creation.

Gandhi, Jinnah, Nehru and other top-ranking leaders who were ultimately responsible for the emergence of independent India and Pakistan came from this class, which was among the principal beneficiaries of British rule but that yet ultimately overthrew it. And this happened sooner rather than later very largely because of the patronage and the condescension with which the British treated Indian intellectuals.

If the European settlers are to see the problem of their own position in Africa as well as the difficulties of the Africans around them, it is essential that they should have some group of people to whom they can turn and who really understand the real nature of the problem and who at the same time are sympathetic to their predicament.

Such a group does not exist anywhere at the present time. Nor can it exist until a great deal more is known about the social pressures and the effects of 'culture shock' upon the European settlers. Unfortunately virtually no practical research into these human problesm has been done at all. British social scientists in the universities or when attached to the Colonial Office have, as in so many other scientific fields, concentrated their efforts on the theoretical rather than the practical. They have undertaken endless research and used thousands of man hours, even man years, making repetitive studies into kinship laws of this or that African tribe, analyzing marriage customs, principles of inheritance and succession. All their efforts have been directed towards the Africans who wear loin-cloths and who still reveal shreds of tribal custom. The man who wears trousers, who joins political parties and calls for the eviction of the Europeans, or the problem of the single woman forced to live in the urban areas and practise prostitution have for the most part seemed too practical or possibly in other ways unworthy of their serious consideration.

It is easier to list the things that have to be done than it is to suggest how the necessary changes could be brought about. Yet there are ways and means even if they are unlikely to meet with the approval of very many people, black or white. It is, however, necessary to stress yet again that no satisfactory solution to the present situation can come about, and there can be no hope of a multi-racial state in Central Africa, unless every one of the proposals already listed are implemented. This is not a dogmatic statement but an absolute reiteration of hard realistic fact. It is as essential that Africans should be treated courteously in public as it is that discriminatory legislation should be swept away. It is as important that Africans should be promoted to managerial positions as it is that African trade unions should be accorded the same facilities as are normal in western Europe. Were these various measures to be introduced very soon and while they could still be made as concessions, then Africans would soon stop joining political parties whose prime motive is the eviction of the Europeans.

Many European politicians have recognized this for some time. They know as well as anybody the great merits of universal adult suffrage. But they believe that in Central Africa too many undesirable consequences would result from such a development. Such may or may not be the case, but it is certainly worth remembering that Disraeli met a situation over the franchise question in Britain not dissimilar to what is now happening in Central Africa. In his day the demand for political participation by the masses was becoming very threatening. But of course those Englishmen who had some education were greatly alarmed, for the 'ignorant masses' seemed such an easy prey for the unscrupulous demagogues who claimed to be their spokesmen and to lead them. One can almost hear the elderly statesmen of the day speaking of the 'so-called leaders'. Certainly these leaders appeared as unsavoury to the then ruling classes as do most African leaders to the Europeans in Central Africa today. But Disraeli stole the thunder of the opposition Whigs by extending the franchise even more widely than even the most extreme advocates of the liberal tradition would have dared. And the effect was quite remarkable. The 'two nations' of the day became one. And the politicians of both parties suddenly found how important it was to know how those who voted for them and whose lives they influenced really felt.

Remove racial discrimination, treat the Africans as human beings, throw open the vote. Utopia! It all sounds so simple and so easy. And it would work if one could do it. But here is the problem. How are these measures to be taken? Who is the impartial body that could command sufficient authority and respect to make the necessary changes in time?

I do not believe that there is any possibility whatever that there is any government in Central Africa, either in the form of a federal government or the government of any of the three individual territories that could obtain a mandate from the European electorate to put through such a programme. In the past every measure attempting to remove racial discrimination has been fought and delayed to the last ditch. Nor is it unreasonable to suppose that if the removal of racial discrimination is to be left to the very people whose prejudice has created and maintained a colour bar almost identical with that of the Union of South Africa, then little can change. In any case, the present leaders of both federal and territorial governments have long ago forfeited any hope that Africans would be prepared to accept them even if they were to change their traditional approach quite radically. These leaders are irrevocably associated in the eyes of every thinking African with seven years of federal government, seven years

The End of an Era

in which they have broken promises, indulged in a series of short-sighted policies and frequently resorted to double dealing in their handling of issues relating to African advancement.

If further reasons are to be put forward as to why the implementation of the necessary measures could not be undertaken from within the territory, one could mention two important issues. There is neither the financial resources available to undertake the necessary development nor the knowledge of how it should be done in the particular situation that now exists. Few people realize the vast capital resources necessary to bring backward people forward at a fast, balanced rate. The total national income of Northern Rhodesia, for example, is around a hundred million pounds a year. This sounds impressive for so small a country, in terms of its population. Yet even if every penny of this income were to be devoted to items of African advancement, it would provide but a tiny part of what is needed. Thus, the Kafue flats agricultural project, that will employ some 300 Europeans and about 20,000 African farmers, will cost well over a hundred million pounds to bring into successful operation and it will be many years before it can start to show any profit.

On the score of knowledge and ability to handle the various issues involved, the Rhodesian people and their governments are just non-starters. Their handling of the 1961 constitutional negotiations showed quite clearly that their sole approach, even after the various emergencies of the previous few years, was the mixture as before. No change likely to make any appeal to the African can therefore be expected from this quarter and though the arrangements made with the British Government in 1961 will reduce the help that Britain can give to the Africans, or the extent to which Britain can influence the settlers themselves, in the long run these changes can only bring nearer the day when Africans will rise in their thousands, sabotage roads, bridges and communications and overwhelm the puny white forces by sheer weight of numbers.

The possibility that the British Government or the people of Britain might provide the necessary impartial body capable of guiding Central Africa into the peaceful ways of racial co-operation must also be discounted. No British Government has yet shown itself impartial — a first essential — nor can the United Kingdom, in its present precarious financial state afford the necessary funds. It certainly does not have the necessary knowledge to get to grips with the problem in a practical way as a matter of urgency. Most important of all, perhaps, it could never use force if the legitimate interests of the settlers were threatened. For whatever the rights or wrongs of the situation, the world today will not tolerate armed pressure used against people emerging from colonial status.

For too long the major political parties in Britain have used the situation in Central Africa for their own political ends and they have given the impression that they are far more concerned with scoring debating points off each other than in providing constructive ideas when questions of the federation have been debated. As Lord Fisher, when Archbishop of Canterbury, remarked in the House of Lords during the debate on the Devlin Report, 'Where we ought to be able to speak with one voice of wisdom to Central Africa, we find ourselves in the lamentable situation of speaking with two.'

Neither party can claim a particularly brilliant record in the handling of Central African affairs or in plans for the future status of the territories. The Labour party have been the most consistent but it is difficult to see how, if Africans are given the power that Socialists believe they should have, that the Europeans will be able to continue an effective body within the Federation or whatever form of territorial grouping emerges.

The Conservatives have been less consistent if perhaps more practical. Had they spoken at the time federation was proclaimed in 1953 as Mr Macmillan spoke in Cape Town in 1961 they would have caused a major revolution, indeed a turning point, in the destinies of Central Africa. But unfortunately, at the time of federation they threw their weight on the side of the European settlers and the Africans turned to the Labour party as their ally. Since then the winds of change have driven Tories from one side to the other. For a time it looked as though they had forsaken the settlers. They recognized that African advancement could only come about if European standards of living were to fall. No doubt the importance of trade with the Afro-Asian block and the large preponderance of coloured people in the Commonwealth all played their part in bringing about this change of heart. But the idea was short lived and as proposed constitutions succeeded proposed constitutions in 1961, it became clear that settler pressure groups were exercising their old ascendency. The Tories failed to understand the significance of the winds of change in Africa, a phrase they had themselves coined. For change is not a new phenomenon in Africa. It has been the order of the day ever since the cry *Ex Africa semper aliquid novi* rang through the debating chambers of the Roman Senate two thousand years ago.

Even if a British Government, of any complexion, were to discard all previous sectional loyalties, and resort to the desperate expedient of rescinding the Federation's Constitution, as was done in the cases of both Nova Scotia and British Guiana, there would still be little prospect of success. When federation was first proposed such a step might have succeeded. But now it is too late. Both African and European settlers, if for very different reasons, have lost confidence in Britain and would oppose both by force and other means any inter-

The End of an Era

ference in the struggle in which they have both become so deeply and irrevocably involved.

If the situation is unlikely to right itself internally, without Africans having to resort to force (it is interesting that the Europeans always claim that Africans use violence whereas they use force), and if Britain has lost the authority and the respect necessary for her to undertake the necessary reforms, then there is only one remaining possibility. The United Nations would have to undertake the work. Such a move, if it could be manoeuvred, would solve some of the problems overnight. The United Nations is certainly a more impartial body than Britain could ever be, even though a large proportion of the member countries would certainly give the Africans the benefit of any doubt that might arise. But if the Europeans are philosophical about this and remember that they have had a long and a good innings, they can still draw comfort from the fact that if the United Nations is to make available the necessary funds, then white people will certainly have to remain and ensure the effective utilization of those funds for many a long year. Central Africa, after all, lags far behind most African territories in the wealth of its indigenous talent. All the African doctors, lawyers, engineers and economists could be counted on the fingers on two hands.

The United Nations is also the only body that could effectively safeguard the legitimate rights of either race. In practice, of course, this would mean safeguarding the legitimate rights of the Europeans. Primarily, these are in the fields of property, private lives and pensions. Only the United Nations could maintain armed forces in the Federation and these forces would probably never be used. But their presence would ensure that in the early days of the Africans gaining political power and before the sense of responsibility had emerged that must come with executive authority, there would be no acts of folly, barbarism, revenge or misdirected exuberance.

There need be no loss to Britain in such a development. It would, of course, be a major change and no doubt some die-hard members of the settler lobby would see the demise of Empire and of British prestige. But it would be in line with the times and certainly there would be more gains than losses. Chief of these gains would probably be in the field of trade. The Central African market is potentially enormous. It is not so much the numerical significance of the population as their latent wealth and the vastness of their needs. Thus, if every house in Central Africa were to be fitted with a tap, running water and electricity, to mention only minor obvious eventualities, it would fill the order books of every British manufacturer of these products for years.

It is true that other countries would try and capture some of the market. But Britain has enormous advantages of experience, language and tradition. We are well established there and far ahead of any competitors. If we have the courage to accept the new political future of the territory and use our engineering skills imaginatively, we could not fail to hold our lead. If, on the other hand, we lack these qualities, then we have no moral right attempting to fence off the territories from our more progressive competitors. In any case, the Africans would never permit us even to try.

The days of Empire, of overseas administration, have gone for good and they should be buried in the pages of history with all the honour that is their due. During all the years that the Empire expanded we always remained essentially a trading nation. This has been our bread and butter and the nature of our population demands that we should continue to live in this way. Our vital interest demands a prosperous Central Africa peopled by progressive and industrious Africans and Europeans. No vital interest is concerned with the maintenance of an outdated order and we would be better served if we were to remember that Disraeli's dictum about Britain having no permanent friends and no permanent foes but only permanent interests, is as valid in the twentieth century as it was in the nineteenth.

Bibliography

Advancement of Africans in Industry, Report of the Commission Appointed to Inquire into the (Dalgleish Report) Lusaka 1944.

Advancement of Africans in the Copper Mining Industry in Northern Rhodesia, Report of the Board of Inquiry into the (Forster Report) Lusaka, 1954.

Ballenden, G. Report on Salisbury's Native Administration. (Salisbury, 1945.)

Batson, E. *The Poverty Line in Salisbury*. (Cape Town, 1945.)

Beames, John. *Memoirs of a Bengal Civilian*. (London, Chatto & Windus, 1961.)

Clegg, Edward. *Race and Politics*. (Oxford University Press, 1960.)

Director of Native Administration, Salisbury Municipality, Annual Reports of. (Salisbury, 1946-51.)

Disturbances in the Copperbelt, Northern Rhodesia, 1935, Report of the Commission Appointed to Inquire in the. (Lusaka, 1935.)

Disturbances in the Copperbelt, Northern Rhodesia, 1940, Report of the Commission Appointed to Inquire into the. (Lusaka, 1940.)

Epstein, A. L. *Politics in an Urban African Community*. (Manchester 1958.)

Forster, E. M. *A Passage to India*. (Kingfisher, 1924.)

Grey, Richard. *The Two Nations*. (Oxford University Press, 1960.)

Gussman, B. W. *African Life in an Urban Area*. (Bulawayo, 1952.)

—— 'Industrial Efficiency and the Urban African'. (*Journal of the International African Institute*, Vol. XXIII, 1953.)

—— 'Problems of Adjustment in British Central Africa'. (*Journal of the Institute of Differing Civilizations*, Vol. IX, 1959.)

Hellmann, E. Rooiyard. *A Sociological Survey of an Urban Native Slum Yard*. (Rhodes-Livingstone Paper No. 13, 1949.)

Legislative Assembly Debates, Southern Rhodesia. (Salisbury.)

Legislative Council Debates, Northern Rhodesia. (Lusaka.)

Lewin, J. *The Colour Bar in the Copper Belt*. (Johannesburg, 1941.)

MacCrone, I. D. *Race Attitudes in South Africa*. (Witwatersrand University Press, 1937.)

—— 'Factors Affecting the Attitude of White and Black in South Africa.' (*South African Journal of Science*, Vol. XXVII, 1930.)

McNamee, J. P. Report on Native Urban Administration in Bulawayo. (Bulawayo, 1948).

Mason, P. *The Birth of a Dilemma*. (Oxford University Press, 1958.)

Mnyanda, B. J. *In Search of Truth*: a Commentary on Certain Aspects of Southern Rhodesia's Native Policy. (Bombay, 1954.)

Native Policy in East Africa, Memorandum on (the Passfield Memorandum). (Cmd. 3573, 1930.)

Orde-Brown, G. St. J. *Labour Conditions in Northern Rhodesia*. (Col. No. 150, 1938.)

—— *The African Labourer*. (Oxford University Press, 1933.)

Perham, Marjorie. *The Psychology of African Nationalism*. (Optima, March, 1960.)

Report of the Southern Rhodesian Convention. (Salisbury, 1960.)

Roux, E. *Time Longer than Rope*. (London, 1948.)

Sanger, Clyde. *Central African Emergency*. (Heineman, 1960.)

Stanford, J. K. (Editor). *Ladies in the Sun: the Memsahibs' of India, 1780-1860.* (Galley Press, 1962.)

Sunkler, B. *Bantu Prophets in South Africa.* (London, 1948).

Tredgold, Sir Robert. Report of the Commission to Investigate the Grievances which gave rise to the Strike amongst African Employees of the Rhodesia Railways. (Salisbury, 1946.)

Wilcox, R.R. Report on a Venereal Disease Survey of the African in Southern Rhodesia. (Salisbury, 1949.)

Wilson, Godfrey. *An Essay on the economics of Detribalization in Northern Rhodesia.* (Rhodes-Livingstone Papers No. 5 and 6. Livingstone, 1941-2.)

Index

Abadan, 24
Accra Conference, 120
Advanced Africans, 99, 141 et seq.
African advancement, 119, 121, 127, 131
African Affairs Board, 142
African Congress, 159
African culture, 49, 50
African leaders, 37, 133, 135, 136, 137, 165
America, 115
Ancestors, 66
Anthropology, 10, 130
Avoidance practices, 83

Banda, Dr, 123, 135, 157
Banda, John, 157
Beadle Inquiry, 158
Beit Trustees, 13
Benson, Sir A., 134
Boers, 26, 27, 28, 41
Boycotts, 159
Bride Price (see lobolo)
Britain, 115, 171 et seq.
British, in South Africa, 27 et seq.
Bulawayo, 30, 32, 38, 40, 77, 94, 99, 126, 128, 129
Burial Societies, 153
Burma, 15, 25
Burombo, 135
Byron, 117

Canterbury, Archbishop (see Fisher)
Car Key Parties, 117, 118
Central Africa, 25, 26 et seq., 47, 48, 52, 53, 69, 76, 77, 85, 113, 115, 120, 125, 137, 141, 144, 160, 162, 164 et seq.
162, 164 et seq.
Central African Examiner, 123, 134
Charity, 21, 24, 140
Chequers, 123
Chidzero, B., 122
Chiefs, African, 56, 63, 134
Chikerema, R., 123
Children, African urban, 78
Chipembera, Mr, 160
Chitepo, H., 125
Christianity, 92 et seq., 154
Churchill, Sir W., 69

Civil Commissioner, 126
Civil Service, 142, 163, 165
Clegg, E., 126
Clutton-Brock, G., 137
Colonial Office, 29, 169
Colour Bar (see Exclusiveness)
Commissioner for Native Labour, 98
Conformity, African, 55, 63
Conservative Party, 173
Conservatism, African, 55
Copper Mines, 40, 114, 116, 130, 131, 157
Cost of Living, African, 107, 108, 110
Coward, Noel, 23
Cromer, Lord, 15
Cruelty, 64, 65
Culture, 43, 44, 49
Culture Shock, 42 et seq., 68

Daily Telegraph, 131
Death Customs, African, 83, 84
Delinquency, African, 144
Detribalization, 36, 53, 66
Devlin Report, 172
Devonshire Declaration, 10, 36, 158
Discrimination, 40
Disraeli, 170, 174
Divorce, 79
Domestic Servants, 110, 111
Drinking, African, 86, 87

Education, African, 80, 89 et seq.
Efficiency, African, 111 et seq.
Egypt, 18, 24
Equilibrium, 63
European Mine Workers' Union, 37
Example, 125, 137
Exclusiveness, European, 17, 18, 19, 22, 24, 25, 120, 123, 126, 140

Family Life, African, 57 et seq., 78, 79
Fathers, African, 83
Federation of African Welfare Societies, 110
Fisher, Lord, 123, 172
Fitzpatrick, B. B., 129
Force, 131, 158 et seq.
Forster, E. M., 17
Fort Victoria, 118

178 *Out in the Mid-day Sun*

Franchise, 132, 163

Germany, 165
Gezira Club, 19
Ghana, 25
Gordon, General, 16

Hanley, Gerald, 17
Health, African, 88
Health Department, 40
Home, Lord, 132
Homes, system of allocating, 84
Hospitality, African, 109
Hospitals, African attitude to, 89
Housing, African, 69 *et seq.*
Huggins, Sir G. (see Malvern)
Hypocrisy, 136, 137

Immigrants, post-war European, 48
Imitation, 51
Incentives, 63, 102, 103
India, 15, 16, 17, 19, 25, 65, 164, 168
Indian Civil Service, 19, 20
Individualism, 55, 66
Industrial Conciliation Act, 102
Industry, 21, 165
Inefficiency, African, 96
Inequality, 39
Inhumanity, 32 *et seq.*
Initiative, 64
Institute of Race Relations, 14

Justice, early European, 32 *et seq.*

Kaffir Beer, 87
Kafue Flats, 171
Katilungu, L., 167
Kaunda, L., 163
Kennan, G., 90
Kenyatta, J., 134
Kipling, R., 19, 22
Kitchener, Lord, 15, 16
Kitchens, African, 82
Kitwe, 121

Labour Party, 172
Labour Recruiters, 97
Labour turnover, African, 87
Land Apportionment Act, 31, 122
Law, African, 63
Leisure, African, 85 *et seq.*
Leisure, European, 114 *et seq.*
Lessing, Doris, 17
Liberalism, dangers of, 17
Livingstone, David, 66

Lobengula, 29
Lobolo, 58
London Missionary Society, 149

MacDougall, T., 118
MacCrone, Professor, 41, 51
McNamee, J., 72, 77, 99, 126
Makarios, Archbishop, 134
Malnutrition, 146
Malvern, Lord, 131, 132, 141
Manners, European, 18, 22, 23, 124, 140, 164, 167
Marriage, African (see also Polygamy), 59, 66, 78 *et seq.*, 145
Mason, P., 14, 32, 124, 128
Massacre Plot, 119
Matabele, 29, 31, 39, 64
Mau Mau, 160
Methodist Church, 89
Middle Class Africans, 84, 141, 168
Migrant Labour, 111, 112
Milner, Lord, 15, 35
Miscegenation, 31, 41, 111
Missions, 92, 93, 137 *et seq.*, 154
Mlimo, 155
Misunderstanding, 51
Monckton Commission, 133
Money, African attitude to, 61, 92, 102 *et seq.*
Monetary economy, 53, 66
Montgomery, Lord, 23
Moussadeq, 24, 134
Municipal Act, 30

Nationalism, 9, 69, 136
Native Affairs Department, 51, 127, 128, 129, 151, 152
Ndola, 118
Nehru, P., 16, 23
Nigeria, 25
Nkana, 37, 127
Nkomo, J., 135, 137
Northern Rhodesia, 29, 35, 36, 37, 70, 76, 101, 107, 114, 118, 121, 125, 130, 132, 133, 134, 142, 152, 157, 159, 161, 164, 167, 171
Nyandoro, G., 123
Nyasaland, 38, 39

Old people, African, 62
Orde-Browne, G. St. J., 97
Overcrowding, 74

Paramountcy, 10
Parents-in-Law, 83

Index

Parliament, 65
Parochialism, 45, 52, 53, 120
Partnership, 10, 122, 130, 131
Pass Laws, 76, 77
Passmore, Lord, 10, 36
Perham, Marjorie, 158
Persia, 24
Personnel Managers, 130, 166
Pioneer Column, 29
Police raids, 76, 77
Polygamy, 20, 60, 81, 82
Population, African, 70 et seq., 77, 78
Power, 159
Press, Rhodesian, 120
Privilege, 164
Productivity, African, 113
Promised Land, 27, 28
Prostitution, African, 75, 76, 88
Public Health Act, 73
Punctuality, African, 49

Reading, 86
Regression, 46, 52
Religion, African, 56, 66
Restrictive Legislation, 30, 31
Revenge, 13, 161
Rhodes, C., 26, 29, 31, 40, 130
Rhodesia Herald, 122
Rhodesian Selection Trust, 14

Salisbury, 129
Samkanga, S., 122
Sanitation, 88
Savanhu, J., 122
Saving, African, 103
Separatist Churches, 154 et seq.
Settlers, 31, 32, 33, 36, 37, 40, 48, 53, 126, 127, 130
Seventh Day Adventists, 138
Sex, African, 79, 87 et seq.
Sex, European, 117
Sharpville, 38
Skokiaan, 87
Slavery, 97
Smuts, J., 38
Societies, African, 151
South Africa, 26 et seq., 100, 170
Southern Rhodesia, 10, 29, 31, 36, 39, 40, 101, 107, 121, 127, 129, 131, 132, 133, 134, 135, 141, 142, 143, 151, 155, 157, 158, 159

Spaciousness, 118
Sport, European, 117, 121
Star Chamber, 131
Status, 55, 61, 62, 63
Standard of Living, African, 107 et seq.
Standard of Living, European, 114 et seq.
Stereotyping, 45, 47, 52, 53, 64, 114
Storrs, R., 15
St Paul, 81
Strikes, 37
Sublimation, 147
Sudan, 15
Supervision of Africans, 90, 100

Taxation in Britain, 115
Times, The, 137
Todd, G., 132, 140, 142
Town Planning, 79
Traders, African, 147 et seq.
Trade Unions, African, 107, 156, 167
Trade Unions, European, 131
Trade Union Organization, 166
Trek, Great, 27
Tribal Life, 54 et seq.
Tsolo, 86

Umtali, 135
United Nations, 39, 173
University College of Rhodesia, 122
Urban Areas Act, 102
Urbanization of Africans, 35 et seq.

Venereal Disease, 37, 89
Victoria, Queen, 15
Victorianism, 48, 52

Wages, African, 106, 107
Welensky, Sir R., 123, 141, 159, 161
Welfare, 140
Whitehead, Sir E., 123
Wife, role of African, 79 et seq.
Wilson, G., 76
Women, African, 58 et seq., 75, 76, 95
Women, European, 52
Work, African attitude to, 61 et seq.
Woodruff, P., 17

GEORGE ALLEN & UNWIN LTD

London: 40 Museum Street, W.C.1

Bombay: 15 Graham Road, Ballard Estate, Bombay 1
Buenos Aires: Escritorio 454-459, Florida 165
Calcutta: 17 Chittaranjan Avenue, Calcutta 13
Cape Town: 109 Long Street
Hong Kong: F1/12 Mirador Mansions, Kowloon
Ibadan: P.O. Box 62
Karachi: Karachi Chambers, McLeod Road
Madras: Mohan Mansions, 38c Mount Road, Madras 6
Mexico: Villalongin 32-10, Piso, Mexico 5, D.F.
Nairobi: P.O. Box 12446
New Dehli: 13-14 Asaf Ali Road, New Delhi 1
São Paulo: Avenida 9 De Julho 1138-Ap. 51
Singapore: 36c Prinsep Street, Singapore 7
Sydney, N.S.W.: Bradbury House, 55 York Street
Toronto: 91 Wellington Street West